Sixty Candles
Reflections on the Writing Life

By Members of the
American Society of Journalists and Authors
On the Occasion
of the
60th Anniversary of
American Society of Journalists and Authors
1948–2008

American Society of Journalists and Authors
New York, New York
2008

iUniverse, Inc.
New York   Bloomington   Shanghai

For the most up-to-date information on iUniverse prices and policies, please call or visit our Web site; iUniverse books may be ordered through booksellers or by contacting:

iUniverse
1663 Liberty Drive, Suite 200
Bloomington, IN 47403
www.iUniverse.com
1-800-Authors (1-800-288-4677)

ISBN-13: 978-0-595-50879-2 (pbk)
ISBN-10: 0-595-50879-0 (pbk)

Printed in the United States of America
Bloomington, Indiana

This book is printed on acid-free paper.

Table of Contents

From the President of ASJA

ASJA turns 60 this year ... almost old enough to collect Social Security! And yet, our organization is far from ready for retirement. To the contrary. Membership is up to an all-time high (nearly 1,400) and continues to grow. Member involvement—on committees, on the online forum, at the annual conference—is stronger than ever. The newsletter and website and events such as personal pitch just get better and better. Most importantly, ASJAers across the nation continue to generously support each other with market information, career tips, making connections, and so much more.

Personally, I can't even imagine how my career—how my *life*— would have been different had I not joined ASJA 13 years ago. I know many of you feel the same way.

This book is a wonderful read and a great testament to our favorite club ... where it's been over the past 60 years, where it is today, and where it may be headed over the years to come. Wherever that may be, I'll happily be a part of it. And I hope you will, as well.

Happy Anniversary, ASJA!

Russell Wild

From the CEO/President of Author Solutions, Inc.

On behalf of iUniverse, I'd like to extend my congratulations to the American Society of Journalists and Authors in recognition of sixty years of service and support of writers, editors and the publishing community.

iUniverse is happy to have played a role in the publication of this book which so vividly pays tribute to ASJA, and in appreciation of our publishing alliance we're pleased to provide copies to all of you. Through this volume, we celebrate the many writers who have published new and out-of-print books through ASJA Press.

We look forward to sixty more years of success for the ASJA and our continued involvement with your publishing efforts.

Best wishes,

Kevin Weiss
President/CEO
Author Solutions, Inc.

Editor's Note

W hen I agreed to edit this book, I didn't know what I was in for.
Literally—there was no sense of what it would be. There was an
occasion: the 60th anniversary of the American Society of Journalists
and Authors. And there was a precedent: *Still Writing After All These
Years*, the 50th anniversary publication. And I had a bit of a personal
motivation, having been introduced to ASJA by Boo Herndon, my
writing mentor, who was one of the early members of the organization,
back when it was called the Society of Magazine Writers. Still, the
biggest job was to figure out what this book ought to be.

I spent some time brainstorming with Alex Owens, recently
returned to the directorship of the organization, bringing with her a long
institutional memory. She pulled out old photographs, old directories,
and old newsletters, and I started approaching the task like a historian.
I got drawn into the spirit of the organization by reading the fading,
typewritten-and-mimeographed newsletters from the 1950s.

Plus ça change, plus c'est la même chose became my chosen theme,
because these newsletters, although from a different era, seemed so
familiar. The contents were the same: market report, organizational
get-togethers, members' publications. Sure, there were details that
showed how things had changed. *Today's Woman* magazine, read a 1952
newsletter, addressed readers who "are mostly college graduates, so
are ambitious in their own right, and also have made a transference of
ambitions to their husbands' careers." *Nation's Business* went to a "busy,
successful" male reader with "a grown family, many productive years
ahead of him"—and an income of "over $12,000." Those were the days
that Boo Herndon used to tell me about, the days of *Cue* and *Coronet* and
the *Saturday Evening Post*, when—as *Saturday Review* editor Norman
Cousins was quoted as saying in the October 1955 newsletter—"the most
critical shortage in America" was information. Yes, those were the days.

Amazingly, the dollar prices for articles were not all that different
from ours today. *Today's Woman* paid $750, "sometimes higher," for
a story "that people will talk about." *Nation's Business* paid $500 to
$1,000 for a feature. *Time* paid $1,000 for a profile, $250 of the total
on acceptance. Plenty of us freelancers today would be happy for such a
deal—and such a byline.

As I read the early newsletters, names of mythic proportion became personalities. Llewellyn Miller, for example. The newest of ASJA members may not know the name, but the Writers Assistance Fund for years was named the Llewellyn Miller Fund. She—yes, she, as Alex informed me—was the newsletter editor for years, and her chipper, wry personality comes out on every page.

So for a while this book was going to be an archive of past ASJA publications, and then it was going to be a record of the ASJA people who had faded into the past. But each of those plans required hours of research and writing time that I just didn't have. I was baffled. I was blocked. The book just wasn't happening, and time was marching on.

Then I got a prod from fellow member Lisa Stockwell. "What's up with the anniversary booklet?" she emailed me from California. And all of a sudden the book was a collaboration. "This is an organization of writers," Lisa said. "Why don't we get them to write it?" Brilliant idea. With the help of Alex Owens and the wonders of email, we put out the call . . . and the rest is (about to become) history.

Contributions came in from 155 ASJA members—young, old, and in between; past presidents and just-joiners; veteran writers and eager upstarts. We agreed to give special placement to the two founders of the Society of Magazine Writers still with us. Norman Lobsenz sent me his piece—in delightfully old-fashioned hard copy—and Don Kirk kindly visited Murray Teigh Bloom. Alex Owens fielded many a question, passed along submissions to me, and drummed up advertisers. Designers at AuthorHouse, of note Jenn Handy and Lauren Allen, turned the manuscript into a book. In other words, this publication could not have been done without the contributions of many.

Lisa and I did our very best to collect up all contributions and treat them kindly, but to anyone out there who finds that we did not include a submission you sent or we misedited your writing, we apologize. We earnestly tried, and it was a labor of love and devotion to this organization. I believe the final product reflects ASJA for what it is: a thriving community of quirky and lovable characters, every one of them with something to say.

—*Susan Tyler Hitchcock*

Chapter 1
Our Founding Members

Sixty Years of Freelancing

How do you sum up sixty years of freelancing? One way, I guess, is to begin at the beginning, which is when I was about ten years old and an aunt gave me a book called *The Boy's Book of Journalism*, because even then I was foolish enough to want to be a newspaper reporter. (I still have that book.) As a present when I graduated from elementary school, I got a Smith-Corona portable typewriter, which I learned to use by trying to write a science-fiction novel. (That manuscript, fortunately, has been lost.)

Then I worked on my high school weekly, college daily, got my degrees from NYU and Columbia Graduate Journalism school, and—finally—got a real job on *Newsday* in 1940 when it began publication. Moved to rewrite on the *N.Y. Post*, the copydesk of the old *N.Y. Mirror*, edited several magazines, and finally decided to become an honest man—a permanent fulltime freelance writer.

Do I regret that choice? Well, sometimes, when I think that I might have broken the Watergate story, or written the Great American Novel. In retrospect, I believe I've not only done better, but achieved more, and had a heck of a lot more fun. Here are some of the fun things:

— I've had assignments all over the U.S., as well as overseas: to Germany, Greece, Africa, Scandinavia, Barbados. Of course that was in what I fondly recall as the Golden Age of freelancing, when etditors had the moxie to approve such assignments.

— I've interviewed fascinating folks—movie stars, the Queen of Iran, Jonas Salk, Jack Nicklaus, dozens of married and divorced couples (family relations was my specialty), and, for a series on newlyweds, I chatted with six very religious young couples about their wedding nights.

— I was probably the first person allowed to use the word "orgasm" in a major women's magazine. Back in the day you couldn't even use "pregnant" in an article.

More important than fun was the sense of freedom—no bosses, no time-clocks, etc. Of course. it was not really freedom, but rather the illusion of freedom. We were always working; we had dozens of bosses (every editor we worked for); we had deadlines; and we were never sure when the assignments would come and the checks received.

With freedom came a complementary sense of accomplishment, whether it was selling an idea, cracking a major market, writing a book, getting an award. Whatever it was, it was all our own doing, from the first blank page to the final "30." Were I to name my personal proudest accomplishment, it would be to have taken part in the founding of the Society of Magazine Writers, to have helped build it through the early years, to have served as its president, and to see it grow into today's ASJA.

As the years pass I think of the men and women, both my fellow-writers and my editors, who were colleagues at first but became close friends. We were a small group, only a couple of dozen in the beginning years, but it was that very intimacy that drew us close, even though we were competing for assignments. Their names would mean little to most of you, and except for one or two all are gone to whatever passes for writer heaven. I still miss them.

Last word: Never lose faith in freelancing. It is a tough business, and not getting easier to survive in these electronic times. Yet somewhere along the way each of us has learned to have faith in our skills and in our selves. How else could I—or could we—ever have dared to become a freelance writer in the first place?

Looking back from the vantage point of being 89 years old, I can whole-heartedly say:

"I wouldn't have missed it for anything."

— *Norman M. Lobsenz*
   Redondo Beach, California

Murray Teigh Bloom, co-founder and former president of ASJA, remains in good health at 91. No longer writing, he revived impressions of ASJA and a career in magazine writing in a conversation with Donald Kirk at his home in a retirement community in North Branford, Connecticut.

Question: What led you to want to found ASJA 60 years ago?

Answer: It was a realization among a few of us that non-fiction had replaced fiction in the magazines. You could organize yourselves so you were not abused by editors and publishers. We felt it was time we had an organization to speak up for us since there was a turnaround primarily to non-fiction.

Q: What were you doing, for whom were you writing, and how did you get into the business?

A: *Collier's, Saturday Evening Post, Liberty, This Week, American Weekly*—I was writing for a bunch of them. I wrote too many articles, don't ask me to remember them. I wrote a few hundred magazine articles. I began with the old *New York American*. I was a campus correspondent. I went to Columbia Journalism School and Columbia College.

Q: How helpful was ASJA in advancing the interests of non-fiction writers?

A: ASJA was very effective. It was badly needed and came along at the right time. When we were together, we realized what power we had. It was a great thing. We were no longer subject to such abuses. It is the only writers' organization, and it remains alive all these years.

Q: How has the business evolved and what special problems to writers face these days as a result of the rise of other media, notably TV and the internet?

A: TV is free, and magazines cost money. You can't compete with TV. I haven't gone online. I never look at the Internet. I never went that far. I don't have the apparatus.

Q: Has ASJA kept up with the needs and pressures facing non-fiction writers?

A: I am no longer on the board of ASJA, but it's the only organization if you're serious about writing for magazines. It's a very tough business. It's a much different business than it was in my day. It takes much more grits and guts to survive than it did then.

Q: What are you reading and looking at on TV these days?

A: I get *The New York Times*, the *New Republic*. I look at *Reader's Digest* because I used to write for them. The Times takes half a day to get through. I watch "60 Minutes," look at Discovery and the National Geographic channels. A writer's curiosity is almost insatiable. You try everything.

Q: How do you look back on your own writing – your favorite topics or assignments?

A: I was there at the right time. The fees were good. It was a great time to be a magazine writer. I did so many, they lose their identity. That's the real problem. I wasn't a specialist. I was a generalist. I can't remember.

Q: How did you make the transition from newspapers to magazines?

A: I worked for the *American* and then the *World-Telegram*. That was a good paper, good writers, good editors. It's a quantum jump when you move from daily reporting to magazine writing. Not every reporter can make that jump. There are fewer opportunities today than in my day, and you have to hit it early. Otherwise it's very difficult to survive. It's so much tougher now.

Q: How difficult was it for you?

A: It was a good field to be in in those days. There wasn't that much stress. It wasn't that hard to be a free-lancer.

Q: How are you doing, and what's your daily routine?

A: For my age, I really marvel at my health. I get around. I don't get any shots. I have my eyesight. I have my hair. I'm very lucky. I try to walk a mile a day. I'm in good shape.

Q: How about your family?

A: I have two daughters and grandchildren. They live around here. At least they're not in Hong Kong or San Francisco. I used to live on King's Point, Long Island. We had a lovely home. My wife passed away. Those are her hats. *(Two hats hang on each side of a large mirror in his bedroom.)*

Q: Any final reflections on your own career—and on ASJA?

A: I had a good life. I was quite lucky. It was a good business in its day. ASJA was badly needed. It came at the right time. We did a good job for our members. We had a lot of good writers.

Chapter 2
Becoming a Writer

I have to thank Lorna.

I don't remember her last name, but I do remember that she was a blond trophy wife in Pacific Heights. I remember she let me drive her black Mercedes. I remember calling my boyfriend on her honest-to-God car phone and telling him as much. I remember when she cried to me about her marriage—over Pad Thai.

When I met her, I was an intern at San Francisco. I fact-checked ("did you mean 'meatball'?") and wrote 65-word previews about galleries (trompe l'oeil, sprezzatura). I came in three days a week. I had my very own cubicle. They didn't pay me. They didn't even give me a bus pass.

It was because they didn't pay me that I worked for Lorna: She wanted to make it big on QVC with an interior decorating kit-in-a-box. Problem, though: She was very pretty, but she was very dyslexic, and couldn't write copy; I knew nothing about interior design. I sat at her desk for months and corrected spelling. She rambled, and I recorded. When she started crying, I stopped jotting.

I was 22, and she had blind faith in my words.

I didn't realize it then, but she gave me my first freelance gig. It wasn't the writing I dreamed of (say, turning the letter "d" to face forward). Things got worse (moving boxes at ad agencies) before they got better (research job at Health). But Lorna paid me to write, and my writing went out into the world, and touched. Someone. That's the most any of us can ask for.

— *Evelyn Spence*
Boulder, Colorado

I backed into writing about Louisiana history and culture—what is now defined as my platform—without much appreciation that I was developing a niche.

I had majored in English and minored in history at a woman's college too small to offer journalism, and so fell into freelance feature writing a decade after graduation. Freelancing was one part of a full life that required juggling the schedules of a busy husband, three young children and various obligations because of and despite them. But it was my definition of me.

A friend of the family who was a local history buff began taking us on outings and adventures—a hike along the Mississippi River levee or at a nearby Civil War fort and park, canoeing in bayous and swamps not far from home, as well as to other local places I had barely noticed.

Soon I realized that stories about such outings were missing from the local newspaper and began to offer them in addition to the freelance pieces I was contributing on the arts, food, and people. Then I broadened my list of publication credits because, I had realized, south Louisiana was very colorful and interesting to others, too. Eventually, this led to three nonfiction books, the last two strictly focused on profiles of places in my area.

I like being recognized for my specialty but I very much enjoyed stumbling about, unfocused, without a platform. I loved the freedom of exploring where my curiosity took me. And, after 35 years, that's still what I most like about freelance writing.

— *Mary Ann Sternberg*
  Baton Rouge, Louisiana

Twenty-seven years ago, I had a miscarriage. It was a late first trimester loss, the kind of thing that happens all the time to millions of women. Physically, it was nearly a nonevent. But emotionally, it felt profoundly eventful, not a *non* in any sense. For reasons that remain mysterious—I had assiduously avoided creative writing classes in college and believed writing for pleasure sounded about as appealing as vacuuming for fun—I decided to mourn the loss with a poem. It was a simple, unsubtle effort, but I submitted it to *Mothering* magazine anyway. When they published my poem and even sent me a small check, my life as a writer was born.

Twenty-seven years later, "The Miscarriage" is still in circulation, republished numerous times in books and newsletters and on the Web. A caption on one Web site reads: "If I only knew where to find [the author of the poem], I would tell her how much we all care." Well, she found me, and the sentiment is much appreciated. After decades of sweating over syntax and dueling with deadlines, the least slick and most sincerely heartfelt thing I ever wrote has turned out to be the most widely reprinted. There is probably a lesson in there somewhere for me as a writer. More than that, though, there is comfort for me as a mother.

— *Linda Wasmer Andrews*
  Albuquerque, New Mexico

🕯 🕯 🕯

Everyone remembers their "first time" and I certainly do. I was in the Army and stationed in Germany. It was 1984 and the dollar was strong, so travel (and writing about it) became my outlet from military life. I submitted a story about Crete to *Stars & Stripes* and they contacted me to say they wanted to buy it for $50. I couldn't believe that someone might pay me to travel (and write about it), so I've never looked back in more than 20 years of full-time freelance travel journalism.

— *Lynn Seldon*
  Oak Island, North Carolina

When I was starting out freelancing, I went to newsstands looking for magazines that might publish my work. I noticed the large number of true confessions and romance magazines. The stories in these were heavily plotted, written in the first person and unsigned, so readers believed the writer had the experience herself. The main readers of these magazines were women living in small rural towns. They had little excitement in their lives and looked to the magazines for that. It was necessary to give details that made the stories sound real to this audience: Your heart is breaking, but you still have to pick up the children at school and make spaghetti for dinner. Most stories were about unlikely, passionate affairs—with the husband's best friend, his father or brother, the reader's best friend's boyfriend. Ecstasy! But ultimately, the heroine saw the mistake she was making and, in an uplifting finish, went back to her husband. I got lots of mail from readers, saying that "your story made me realize what I was doing and if you had the strength to do the right thing, I can do that, too." I could have had a career in true romance, but I knew I had to go on to more conventional freelancing if I wished to advance. And that is what I did, writing 17 books and countless magazine articles on serious topics. Still, I learned a lot that stood me in good stead when I turned to literary fiction.

— *Lucy Kavaler*
  New York, New York

As a one-time high school English teacher, I've always enjoyed reading and writing, but I came to my career as a freelance writer late in life and serendipitously. Attending classes in 1984 to become a Minnesota Master Gardener required me to pay back in volunteer hours, so I opted to write a newspaper garden column. To learn how to break into magazines, I enrolled in a community college course titled "Writing for Publication," and my instructor just happened to be a member of ASJA. I joined soon after finishing the course. My first sale was $1,000 for an essay about my empty-nest syndrome I sold to a slick New York City–based magazine called *Countryside*. I was ecstatic! Since then I've written for nearly a hundred other magazines, and I wish I'd started down this path much sooner. I hope to continue writing as long as I live because nothing has given me such pleasure, such satisfaction, such a sense of accomplishment. How else would I have been able to travel to Midway Atoll, visit the "Forbidden Island" of Ni'ihau with its owner, a controversial plant conservationist, or stay at luxurious log lodges across the U.S. and Canada?

— *Margaret A. Haapoja*
  Bovey, Minnesota

The Power of Story

Imagine a five year old boy—no brothers or sisters—isolated on a farm two miles from the nearest town (population 626) in central Texas. Less than four feet high and unemployed. Very little reading material, even if he could read. That little cowboy made up a lot of stories. Dead outlaws all over the place.

On the wall in the dining room was a telephone—a big wooden box with a cone receiver and a hand crank to call the operator and tell her the number you wanted. In the country you shared a party line with four to six other people. (We were one long and one short ring).

Then I made a major discovery. The kind that James Hillman speaks of in *The Soul's Code* as the spark that ignites a life's calling. I learned, accidentally at first, then quietly, that you could listen to stories. Miss Dessi lived two more miles down the Calieche Road, but she was only two shorts, and a long away. Her currency was information. And she was one rich woman.

She and her friends expanded my world view, and elevated the quality of my stories. She single-handedly saved a lot of West Texas outlaws from an early death—I had to stay close to the phone.

I still listen to stories, and tell a few of my own, but there are two significant differences. People know I'm on the other end of the telephone. And they pay me to listen.

— *David Krueger, M.D.*
Houston, Texas

The year was 1967. I was a 20-something ex-pat living in Ierapetra on the island of Crete and dreaming of being a published writer. My typewriter had been stolen in London so I hand wrote a query to *Gourmet* for an armchair travel piece about Vasilis' Taverna, a local eatery on the Mediterranean complete with fresh fish, a blind Bouzouki player, and impromptu nightly dancing by the patrons. To my great delight, the pitch earned me a go-ahead on spec. I borrowed a typewriter from an English teacher who was in town and sent my manuscript across the Atlantic to meet its fate. Shortly thereafter, I got an acceptance letter and a check for $300. My career was underway! That acceptance letter, nicely framed, still hangs above my desk today. Looking at it never fails to bring back the giddy sense of triumph I felt when I first tore open the envelope that held the affirmation that my dream had become a reality.

— *Sondra Forsyth*
New York, New York

🕯 🕯 🕯

Nonfiction writing has served me very well during a long career, and I'm thankful a wounding rejection letter set me on that path. In the beginning I imagined myself as a topnotch fiction writer with short story bylines everywhere and the Great American Novel also in the works. With these hopes for the future I submitted what I considered a truly dramatic short story with a well-crafted heroine, Kathy, to a southern magazine. But the letter rejecting the story read: "We're returning your submission because our readers don't like stupid characters, and your character Kathy is stupid."

I got the message on fiction and turned to my first nonfiction with "I Want To Be A Writer," which sold to a soon-to-be-defunct writer's magazine. They paid me with four books on how to write. Oh, well. We all had to start somewhere.

— *Roberta Roesch*
Westwood, New Jersey

I started my writing career at the top. My first published essay was in the *Village Voice* in the 80s, back when it was known for literary quality. Here's how it happened. I was looking for love by advertising in the *Village Voice* personals. I put in an ad that mentioned that I was overweight, a writer, looking for a guy who liked heavy women. I got a response from Ned Sonntag, a comic book illustrator. Ned is what's known as a "fat admirer" but wasn't looking for a date—he was living with someone at the time—he needed a writer who would do a piece about fat fashion for the *Village Voice*. It seems he'd run into Mary Peacock, the editor of the *VV* fashion section, at a party, mentioned that he liked fat women, and she asked him to do a piece on fat fashion. He agreed, only later realizing that he didn't write essays, he wrote for comic books. (Ned was a tad spacey.) So he started looking for a writer and found me through the personals, unpublished but certainly fat. I wrote "Fat Fashion Frustration on Fifth Avenue," Ned illustrated it, brilliantly, and mailed it to Mary. When she found it on her desk, she had no idea where it came from because she'd long ago forgotten talking to Ned; but she published it and I became the *VV* fat fashion writer. That was the best gig I ever had—almost 30 years ago. Mary was the best editor I ever had, we edited every piece together, sitting in front of her computer at the *Voice*. I thought all editors were like her. Boy, was I wrong. It's been downhill ever since.

— *Erica Manfred*
 West Hurley, New York

My mom called my visits to the nursing home Thursdays With Helen. (She never wanted to infringe on anyone's copyright.) We'd jabber mostly about the family, football games, the weather, neighbors, and stuff once in her house. One day, she looked at me with that funny "mother knows best" smile.

"I always knew you'd be a writer," she said.

"What? Was I born with a silver pen in my hand? That must have hurt."

"No, I think it was the time you tried to read me *Peter Rabbit* when you were three. And don't forget the songs. You know, the songs…"

My mind flipped back to being 4 years old, swaying on the swing in the backyard. There, I would sing songs at the top of my tiny lungs about bugs, birds, bees, and bologna. The family story goes that one day I marched into the kitchen and announced, "Someone should write my songs down. Now. They're great." (Remember, this was Tony the Tiger days.)

Truth be told, I knew I'd eventually become a writer, too. It wasn't only my childhood songs. Our house was wall-to-wall books. Dad was an English major; Mom read all the time. I could recite "Gunga Din" and "The Raven" at age 6. In high school, my friends hid their "dirty" books in my locker. They knew if I was hauled into the principal's office, and my parents called in, they'd say, "Hey, she's reading!" Nothing was verboten; every book was sacred.

And for that, I thank my parents not only on Thursday—but every day.

— *Patricia Barnes-Svarney*
Endicott, New York

Back in the early 1960s when I got my first job in journalism at *Philadelphia Magazine*, I was ecstatic. The staff of three hot shot writers was not. They had me pegged as a suburban housewife with no talent who had no place working at the first breakout city magazine in the country. On my first day they took me out to lunch and did everything they could to convince me I wasn't wanted. But I didn't care. I knew I had the right stuff and that they needed me. The editor just sat back with a let-the-chips-fall-where-they may attitude and let them harass me.

I happily made the coffee, organized their filing system and payments, and wrote whatever no one else wanted to. I stuck my nose in the advertising, production, and bookkeeping departments and learned how a magazine worked. Finally I was allowed to write the kind of articles the big boys wrote (as long as I kept making the coffee and keeping the accounts straight).

Many years and magazines later, I realized how lucky I had been to start in a small, disorganized shop where I could learn every part of the business. How valuable all that knowledge was and still is for everything I have done in publishing. I'm not suggesting we go back to those pre-p.c. days, but only that starting your career where you have the opportunity to learn from the ground up can be perhaps humbling, but it can also be one smart move.

— *Nancy Love*
New York, New York

Years ago, my then 9-year-old son got hooked reading R. L. Stine's *Goosebumps* books. The creepy stories didn't have many redeeming literary qualities, but Mark and his buddies raced through the entire series. I wondered if I should be pushing "better" books or if quantity was better than quality. I proposed the topic to *Parenting* magazine and they quickly assigned the story. At that moment freelancing seemed like the ideal job. I could ask national experts to weigh in on my parenting questions.

Freelancing was indeed the perfect job for a number of years until contract hassles outweighed writing satisfaction and the isolation of working from home outweighed the flexibility. I made a career switch to become a preschool teacher. Instead of asking experts all those niggling questions, I became the expert in parents' eyes and needed to answer their questions myself. It was an odd role reversal but I found I enjoyed passing on my experience. I just completed the manuscript for my first book—a preschool curriculum guide to be published by Gryphon House in Spring 2009. My career path, aided by ASJA colleagues all the way, gives me goosebumps.

— *Marie Faust Evitt*
  Mountain View, California

The Day That I Was Lionized... Well, Almost

It was 1955, my first freelancing year. Arlene and I (she, 18, my beautiful bride of a week, 30 years before her blockbuster bible *What to Expect When You're Expecting*) were on a two-month Florida writing honeymoon, which considering the number of $5 and $10 wedding gifts from my frugal relatives, direly required refinancing. What, I speculated, could be a better source of technicolorful pieces than the circus' Sarasota winter quarters.

Bullseye! A remembrance of Circus giant Ted Evans appeared as "Requiem for a Giant" in *Show*. And then colorful lion trainer Oscar Konyot appeared. "You should meet John Ringling North," said Oscar after our initial interview. That evening at the Ringling Hotel bar we did. "If you're doing a piece on Oscar," North said, " you really need to get in the lion's cage." I said I'd think about it.

Next morning, Arlene and I walked what felt like the last mile to the lion's den. "That's Juno in there," Oscar said. "She'll like you." Not for breakfast, I hoped, but whatever happened, I wanted this on film. "Ready with the camera?" I asked my bride. "Yes," she said, focusing on Juno and no doubt wondering if she'd be a widow before our honeymoon was over. I hoped her hands weren't shaking.

But Juno wasn't hungry. Oscar was right behind me—out of camera range—stool and whip in hand. And after making sure that my intrepid act had been recorded for posterity ("Arlene, did you get it?"), I backed out slowly, being careful not to trip over the stool. I couldn't wait to get to my Smith-Corona portable (remember them?) to write my profile of Oscar. *Real Magazine* bought it for $350—the $50 being for Arlene's totally-in-focus photo.

— *Howard Eisenberg*
New York, New York

I got my start as a freelancer thanks to a bunch of libidinous felines.

My neighbor had an unspayed white female, which she let roam about freely outdoors. The cat, aptly named Blanche, had a favorite spot: My porch. When Blanche went into heat, she attracted a small army of suitors. At night, their lusty wailing shattered the quiet. I discovered on several occasions upon returning home that tomcats do not take kindly to having their amorous affairs interrupted. The mystery of why Blanche never had kittens only made this ongoing nuisance more confounding. I banged pots and pans, barked like a bloodhound, and complained to my neighbor, all to no avail.

Yet, an upside to this odd and unnerving situation eventually emerged. On a whim, I had signed up for a writing course at an adult-education center. Mining my personal life for material, I wrote a short essay about the cat problem. At the instructor's urging, I submitted the piece to the local newspaper's op-ed page. The $25 check I received in return was less important than the editor's encouragement to pitch more story ideas, which led to a string of assignments. Those clips helped me get a full-time newspaper job, which I quit four years later to freelance full time.

That was 20 years ago. I don't know what became of Blanche and her boys. But I ended up grateful that their passion helped me to discover mine.

— *Tim Gower*
Harwich, Massachusetts

More than 20 years ago, I wrote an essay for a college class and, on a whim, submitted it to the now defunct *Newsweek on Campus*, a publication distributed in university newspapers nationwide. Figuring the odds were slim, I promptly forgot about it. (Besides, it was my senior year and my social life was finally getting good.) A few months later, an editor in New York called to say *Newsweek* wanted to pay me $500 for it. That bought a lot of beer in a small college town in western Massachusetts circa 1986.

From this moment on, I was basically ruined. What better way could there be to make money? I have been a dog walker. I have been a college instructor. I have been a communications director at a major university. But there is never any greater professional thrill than getting word a national publication is going to print my words and pay me for them. Despite kill fees. Despite pay checks that take five months to arrive. Despite occasionally nasty editors (one of whom recently wrote "lame" next to one of my sentences in a revision letter). I get paid to learn. I get to work on projects that I thought were a good idea from the get-go. I get to pick my kids up from school and go to the gym in the afternoon. How many people can say that? So, more accurately, I am thoroughly ruined. But I have come to make my peace with that.

— *Renée Bacher*
   Baton Rouge, Louisiana

Follow Your Feet

My dad was worried about me. Not only did I hate my job at an ad agency, but I also had to dress up daily, with makeup, fluffed-up hair, a suit—and pumps: the only shoe deemed professional enough for my fancy office.

Barefoot is my natural state: as a child in Alabama, I'd left a trail of tossed-off shoes in my wake whenever the weather was warm.

Then one day at my dad's, I kicked off my sandals.

"What's that?" he growled, pointing at a knob on my heel.

"That's called a 'pump bump.'" I lifted both heels to show angry callouses.

He grimaced. "Your feet are becoming disfigured."

I shrugged. "That's what I get for working in an office."

"When are you going to get out of there?"

Daddy never gave advice: he always said I had a good head I could use to figure out my own way. But in the year since my mother died, I had been floundering. My dreams, my ambition were mired in sadness. Much like his.

I wanted to write for magazines. But how?

My dad explained how to start a business, like he had done before I was born. "Line up plenty of customers. Buy a computer. And expect to work harder than you have ever worked."

I was scared. Could I do this?

"If I fail, will you send me care packages?"

"You know I would. But I know I won't have to."

Within months, I had enough magazine work to quit my job. Eventually, my feet went back to normal, and my head followed.

— *JoBeth McDaniel*
Rancho Palos Verdes, California

Faith for the Journey

For years, I ignored the voice in my mind that prompted me to write. Ultimately, I realized I was denying a gift by not fanning my flickering writing passion into flame. When I finally stepped onto the writing path, my pace moved rapidly. With few publishing credits, I attended a writers' conference. Researching the publishers beforehand, I knew my target house. The editor representing that publisher offered only three appointments. With hundreds of conferees, the sign-up process was mass chaos. I prayed. A sea of people parted and I saw the editor's name on the table. I stepped through the gap and signed my name beside the one remaining appointment slot.

When we met, the editor scanned my proposal. Minutes dragged. Without looking up, she instructed me to see a different editor while there. I talked to him the next morning at a breakfast table full of strangers. He stated his skepticism that the subject, suicide, would ever make it through committee. But God performed a miracle as six strangers spontaneously shared their stories of suicide's impact on their lives. Amazed, the editor said, "Five minutes ago, I thought your topic too narrow to consider publishing, but this table is a microcosm of society. There's a need for this book." Several months later, my first book contract arrived.

If I'd continued to deny my calling to write, I'd have missed a blessing. Now I continue my writing journey with faith that the way is paved before me.

— *Candy Arrington*
  Spartanburg, South Carolina

The seeds for my becoming a freelance writer were planted the day I stepped foot into my first post-college job at a public relations firm, even if I didn't know it for another eight years. That's when I met a staffer who'd just returned to work full-time, leaving her three-month-old at home. Yes, I wanted an interesting, satisfying career. But no way was I not going to be around when my as-yet-unborn child (conceived with my as-yet-unknown husband) joyfully took his first toddling step, or tearfully smacked his head on the coffee table. Over time I cast about for a career that met my requirements, including my passion for writing, and freelance magazine work became the obvious conclusion. A few months before my first child was born I stepped out of the office world for good; some 16 years later I look back with approval and appreciation.

Sure, there have been challenging days. I have occasionally gone through the clump and slump periods inherent in the field. I've had to wait for some checks longer than *American Idol* fans have to endure not knowing who'll wear the next crown. And while I always tried to have babysitters watching my kids while I worked, I have had phone interviews interrupted by a child shouting the need to go potty, or slipping in to hang up the phone. (My girlfriend used to take calls in her closet so frequently that she called it her "cloffice.")

In what other careers can you not only command your own flexible hours and still make good money, but feel challenged, fulfilled and, yes, even like you're making a difference to others, at the same time.

— *Meryl Davids Landau*
  Boca Raton, Florida

I must reveal, in 25 words or less, how my writing life began, because…
    …I entered contests; won cash (lots), went on trips (many), sold more major appliances than Sears, and turned a contesting flair into a freelance career.

Instead of 25-word statements like that last one, I now write 25 *hundred* word articles; instead of entering contests, I create and judge them.

I challenged readers of *Games* magazine to write a flattering piece and, through punctuation alone, transform it into disdain.

My example:

Flattery: Dear John, I want a man who knows what love is all about. You are generous, kind, thoughtful. People who are not like you admit to being useless and inferior, John. You have ruined me for other men. I yearn for you. I have no feelings whatsoever when we're apart. I can be forever happy. Will you let me be yours? Gloria

Disdain: Dear John, I want a man who knows what love is. All about you are generous, kind, thoughtful people, who are not like you. Admit to being useless and inferior, John. You have ruined me. For other men, I yearn. For you, I have no feelings whatsoever. When we're apart, I can be forever happy. Will you let me be? Yours, Gloria

Stephen M. Hopkins, a university Director of Choral Activities, put music to my words and sheet music enables choral groups all around the country to sing my song.

I now own this CD:
       DEAR JOHN
       DEAR JOHN
       Lyrcis by Gloria Rosenthal
       Music by Stephen M. Hopkins

— *Gloria Rosenthal*
   Valley Stream, New York

One Idea Away From a Best Seller.

I am a speaker that writes, not a writer that speaks. It is a subtle but distinct difference. I realized somewhat late in my career that speakers who had written books made considerably more money than speakers who didn't, so I decided I had to write at least one. My first three books were Mickey Mouse books, meaning, a bunch of speakers got together and each wrote a chapter. We called it an anthology and we "felt" like authors, acted like authors and quite frankly, sold quite a large amount of books, back of the room. Finally I decided I had to write a book all by myself. It didn't feel quite right to have three anthologies in the market; I really didn't think of myself as an author. My first book was *How to Survive Among Piranhas: Motivation to Succeed.* I self published it but a year later, based on sales, it was picked up by Planeta Publishing Company, the largest Spanish publisher in the world and seventh overall. The book was doing very well but I knew I didn't have a best seller yet. Then, the big idea hit me like a ton of bricks. Out of it came the book *Don't Eat the Marshmallow…Yet: The Secret to Sweet Success in Work and in Life.* It has now been translated into twenty languages and it sold 2 million copies worldwide. It again proves that every writer is just one idea away from a best seller.

— *Joachim de Posada*
   San Juan, Puerto Rico

I began my writing career with stories in the *New York Times*, the *Herald Tribune*, and *Parents*, about our European travels, usually preceded by queries pitching the piece. Most queries brought replies of thanks but no thanks. Then I hit the jackpot. A major magazine invited me in to discuss my story. I was bedazzled. Even more so when they offered what was then an enormous sum for the final piece. "What do you say to $$$?" they asked. Looking back, I am mortified by my response. "I say, you're saints!"

My article bombed, and there were no kill fees in those good old days! But I went on to work at *Good Housekeeping* and publish some children's books, so there's been a happy ending of sorts for me.

— *Dorothy Siegel*
  Fair Lawn, New Jersey

After a few post-college false starts, I walked into the old-fashioned newsroom of a daily home furnishings trade newspaper one spring day and found my calling as a journalist in less than an hour. I was charmed by the battered reporters' desks, each with its own copy spike, and by the managing editor who wore a pencil behind his ear and shouted "COPY" every 15 minutes or so, bringing teenage copy clerks running. Finally, I found a work environment that appealed to me.

I was ill-equipped for the job. When I got my first important assignment, which was to report on "wholesale" furniture showrooms in Manhattan that pretended to offer lower prices than typical retail furniture stores, I called on my academic experience and went to the public library to look up the topic in the *Reader's Guide to Periodical Literature*. I told the managing editor that I couldn't do the story because there were no articles on the topic. He explained to me that reporters usually get their information by interviewing people. He was polite, but his sad-eyed expression showed that he saw little future for me in the news gathering game.

I took the frightening step of going into "the field," risking visits to the showrooms to ask nosy questions; I even went so far as to contact the showrooms' competitors for their point of view. Eventually, I handed in a pretty good article and had the pleasure of seeing my byline on page one. It was a beginning that led to untold numbers of nosy questions in "the field" and a great deal of fun.

— *Barbara Mayer*
  Pound Ridge, New York

Writing from the Deep End of the Gene Pool

Granny wrote constantly in tiny watercolor tablets, her jottings mixed with tiny paintings—history at its most intimate. I was honored to be given one of these tiny tablets at seven.

In boarding school at 14, I wrote home a lot. When letters came back to me with circles and arrows in red from my father, an editor at the *Readers Digest*, I froze. I know with the wisdom of 58 years that he was sincerely trying to help me learn to express myself, seeing something that I was too young to see.

I got over my first experience of writing being "marked up" by my father when I fell in love. My boyfriend suggested I go into the business of ghosting love letters. Instead I timidly wrote for our local newspaper.

Eventually I was asked to write an article for a very prestigious super-yacht magazine. Little did the captain and crew know how nervous I was, since I had never done this before. But the article, my first feature, was a huge success. Breathe.

With hindsight I realize that my words were clear, but they weren't particularly entertaining. My "voice" was fearful of painting artistic and personal pictures as Granny had done. I lived in fear of the circles and arrows in red.

I plunged into the gene pool to infuse my work with Granny's scribbled intimacy, Dad's humor and finesse, and my family culture of finding the right words. Now I have a voice that is the product of three generations, and I am proud to share the gene pool with them.

— *Brooke Cunningham*
  Waitsfield, Vermont

Chapter 3
The Writer's Life

A Net Gain

What a different world this was for writers sixty years ago. Manual typewriters and carbon paper. Long waits while original manuscripts, bound in paper and string, were sent across the country, to editors who worked "8/5," not "24/7." Yes, it's a different world today.

Now, you might email a query and before you can pat yourself on the back, you hear a faint ding bringing rejection at lightning speed. How long would it have taken, if you heard back at all, even just a dozen years ago? Love 'em or hate 'em, computers and the Internet have forever changed the writing world.

We 21st-century writers have a glorious advantage no one could foresee. Technology, especially the Internet, enables a more productive writing experience. We can work anywhere, with instant communication. We are the first generation to know the extraordinary benefits of online research. In minutes, we can find Ethiopian health statistics, the history of the Smithsonian Castle, or the entire text of Oscar Wilde's *De Profundis*. Written while imprisoned in 1895, Wilde received one sheet of pale blue paper from his jailer each day. He not only wrote *De Profundis* in this manner, he was required to hand over each sheet of paper before receiving another. Yet Wilde states: "Of course to one so modern as I am, 'Enfant de mon siecle,' merely to look at the world will be always lovely."

Indeed it is lovely to us, children of our century.

— *Helen Gallagher*
Glenview, Illinois

I was coaching a kids' game in the local rec leagues when a grateful mom took the time to thank me.

"No problem," I said. "I really like doing something for the kids."

"My husband would love to help coach, too," she said. "But he works."

"Well," I said, after a pause. "I work, too."

"Oh, you do?" she said, clearly surprised and a little embarrassed. "I'm so sorry. Somebody told me you were a writer."

— *Tim Harper*
  Ridgewood, New Jersey

☽ ☽ ☽

I just finished a book that I worked on for three years. It took so long because it is an evidence-based book on the psychology behind the relationship between people and their companion animals (aka pets). Consequently, the research, which is 90% of writing, was arduous. There were many, many days when I thought I would not finish, and that I would end my career as a writer in shame. My husband is a psychologist and during one of his professional meetings, I lamented to one of his colleagues, Eric Harris, Ph.D., about my stress and concern about finishing by saying, "Writing is like giving birth to an elephant; it takes so long." His quick response had amazing accuracy born of experience. He said, "Giving birth to an elephant would be easy; all you would have to do is wait." He helped me face a hard truth: Writing takes concentrated effort and time; there is no way out. His comment stuck with me and when I felt dismayed, I would remember that writing is hard work, but the rewards of having written are precious.

— *P. Elizabeth Anderson*
  Arlington, Virginia

After writing nearly 15,000 magazine pieces and 20 books in 52 years, including an E&P best seller, I'm still amused that I also wrote two book manuscripts that were accepted and I was paid thousands for them . . . but they were never published!

Fortunately, I got the rights back. Like other ASJAers, I knew writing was my destiny. It enabled me to interview and glean knowledge from ASJA members and others like James Michener, Alex Haley and Rod Serling. My success came from those willing to share their experiences because, like me, they totally enjoyed a vocation that was also their avocation. Success in writing is in the details; it takes emotion, feeling and empathy to cause readers to weep, laugh and muse.

One of the first pieces I sold for the unbelievably low price of $15 was about a Ringling Brothers Barnum & Bailey clown who lost both legs from diabetes and who, for months, regaled the children's wing of a hospital in an Ohio city. Every day he would painfully put on his clown costume with help from nurses and wheel himself to perform for the children. I spent a half-day with him and I came away a changed person. I knew he was in pain so I asked the obvious: why?

"I'm doing what I do best and I'm so happy I can still do it."

Fifty years later, "Happy" Sinclair's words and photo are still above my desk. I've tried to live up to his standards.

— *Jack Behrens*
Clinton, New York

Unusable

After years of successful freelancing, an editor once called to tell me an assigned article I'd written was "unusable." I plunged headfirst into Kubler-Ross's five stages of grief. A summary:

1. Denial. Obviously, the editor has confused her "accepted" and "unusable" piles. Soon the phone will ring with a call from someone eager to clear up this "misunderstanding."

2. Anger. *My* work unusable? I'd bet money this woman would be among those who passed on the Harry Potter books. Moron.

3. Bargaining. Okay, fine, I'll do the rewrite. And it will be so magnificent, this editor will apologize for ever momentarily doubting my almost God-like talent. (And God, if you make my writing extra great, I will no longer spend hours Googling my name and counting it toward my writing time. Deal?)

4. Depression. I have less than 48 hours to pull off a rewrite of an article that took me the better part of a month to complete. I'd get started, except I can't seem to stop shoving chocolate-chip ice cream down my throat as I repeatedly watch *Titanic*.

5. Acceptance. I review my article and realize something—she's right. The piece I submitted is too technical, not enough heart. I stop perusing the local want ads (I didn't want to learn to drive a semi, anyway) and start writing

The result: My rewrite is accepted. The editor is happy. And I no longer Google my name. (During writing time...) Next project, please.

— *Dena Harris*
  Madison, Wisconsin

Writing as a Sensual Pleasure

I write this as I begin my seventh decade on earth and as someone who has been writing professionally since the 1960s when I became a reporter for a small weekly. Some people become addicted to booze, some to drugs, and some to sex. For me, the addiction was always writing.

Reading always, writing has been the way I have pursued my learning curve through life. It has been a long conversation with myself and with whomever is reading what I have written, either to pay the rent or just to scratch that daily itch that comes from observing the absurdities of the world around me.

In a very real way, I don't really know what I know or what I think until I have written it. I like documentation. I like knowing I can cite a source rather than permit myself to bloviate like some self-intoxicated politician or academic.

If I could no longer write, I would be crippled and would surely die soon after, but what I would miss most is the sheer sensual pleasure of seeing the words leap from my mind to the page.

Let others fulfill themselves in the countless ways that people do. For me, writing is the breath of life. It's better than chocolate, better than a good cigar, better—yes—than sex.

— *Alan Caruba*
   South Orange, New Jersey

While writing several pieces for a little mag called *Florida Retirement Living*, I noticed something was missing. Retirees travel. Right? So why didn't a magazine that was slanted to seniors for over 40 years not print one word on places to see and things to do when they got there? My idea to write a regular column on Florida travel was promptly embraced by the then editor/publisher. Despite it's rather contentious end, it proved to be one of the smartest moves I've made in 20 years of freelance writing.

Before the first *Florida Fun for Few $$'s* column was published in January, 1992, I'd sold about a dozen travel articles, over half of them to national publications. All were on trips I'd paid for out of my own pocket, not too easy for a freelancer. Suddenly, I'm doing a regular stint on assignment, arranging freebies with CVB's around the state that add more markets. Small but steady checks pad my bank account. Photos add more $$s, and one time rights mean multiple sales. The party lasted until May, 1995 when a new editor, himself a travel writer, took over 99% of the magazine. It folded a couple of years later. But I've been making money from what I wrote for that publication ever since.

— *Adele Woodyard*
  Tarpon Springs, Florida

Who ARE Those Happy People?

When I worked in magazine office jobs, I'd see people strolling through the Village in the middle of the day and wonder, Who ARE those people? Don't they have jobs? Then four years ago, I finally went freelance, determined to become one of them.

The first morning I awoke as my own boss, though, was a strange one. I had one assignment, so I sat down and got started. (Slooooowly, mind you. It was Parkinson's Law in action: My work more than expanded to fill the time I was given to complete it...) At lunchtime, I grabbed a *New York Post* and walked to Washington Square Park to breathe in my freedom. But I couldn't relax. I felt like I was breaking an office hours law and was bound to be caught. I had no co-workers to alert where I was; no boss to expect me back.

"Absolutely no one knows where I am right now," I thought. It was a scary feeling I wasn't sure I'd get used to.

Well...I got used to it all right. I now live in Los Angeles, and though work certainly tries to preclude all pleasure, I still force myself to take advantage of things I swore I would: I make my own ours (sometimes the creativity flows at 8 a.m. for 10 hours; sometimes it flows at 8 p.m. for four). And when I'm done cranking my work out, I take breaks, naps, walks and bike rides, and play paddle tennis during the week when courts are actually available.

To anyone who sees me and my fellow writers doing all those things and wondering, "Who are those people? Don't they have jobs?" The answer is: Why yes, we do. We're freelancers. And we have the best jobs on earth.

— *Amy Spencer*
  Venice, California

I've been making my living (such as it is) working with words for almost 38 years now. Is it possible to sum this up in under 250 words? If that's the assignment, of course. I'll stick to the best part of it—the variety. I've been privileged to taste from life's big menu. I've written about pigs in literature, and actual pigs; I've written about hockey, baseball and golf; I've written about writers, composers, businessmen and bellydancers, winemakers, brewers, cooks and cookies (Oreos, to be precise); I've written about Native Americans, buffaloes, history, Harley-Davidsons, about science, UFO's, crime scene investigation, carrier pigeons and Trappist monks.

For assignments I've played golf in Iceland, Australia and China (only three continents to go), I've driven race cars, I've hobnobbed with the rich and the wacky (sometimes simultaneously), I've interviewed some personal heroes (like Pete Seeger and Aaron Copland), and have played golf with Ernie Els and Arnold Palmer. For various articles I've been forced to go whale-watching, play pool, have massages, drink beer, go to the race track, gamble, attend concerts, and go fishing.

The problem is I eventually have to sit down at the desk and write about all this. If that's the hard part, it's the thrilling part, too. It's the fun and challenge of writing that makes all the rest of it happen anyway. Add the hope—and probably original impetus—that one can actually be of some use along the way, and who can complain?

— *Tom Bedell*
  Williamsville, Vermont

For many years, I plotted to write serious narrative nonfiction books that would make me financially independent. Unlikely, I realized, but still...

For my third book, a biography, my proposal generated so much interest that my agent held an auction. I received a large advance from a major publisher. I'm set, I thought. I spent six years researching and writing the book. It received excellent reviews. It sold, but not well enough to earn back the advance.

Only then did I realize the mixed blessing of a large advance. It afforded me enough money to do the book right while more or less supporting my family. But I was now marked as a midlist, money-losing author.

Since then, I have continued writing serious narrative nonfiction books with top-notch publishers. It appears, however, that I will never become self-sufficient financially that way. Back to my current magazine feature deadline, then to the book review due next week...

— *Steve Weinberg*
  Columbia, Missouri

After growing up reading books by early travel writer Richard Halliburton, I dreamed of traveling the world to see its wonders for myself. Like many life paths that take a side-turn, the "hormone age" issued me marriage and a bunch of rowdy kids instead of airline tickets, but I never forgot my dream. When family responsibilities eased—children eventually do grow up—I hit the road.

I'm amazed when I realize how much writing has enhanced my experience of this wonderful world and its myriad cultures. I've written one book, and am working on two others: one a travel memoir that tells what didn't get into the hundreds of travel articles I wrote over the years to editors' specifications.

I'm writing about times when I got locked in the loo at the Catacombs (Rome), got locked out of Shakespeare & Co. (Paris), expected Mariachi and Ballet Folklorico and found the Holiday Inn and the twist (Mexico), got stuck in the mud underneath a limb full of leopard (Kenya), tumbled down an up escalator (Florida), found Gaugin's grandsons (Tahiti, Marquesas), jumped ship in Jakarta (Indonesia), waded through Venice, ate my way across Canada, went naked in Istanbul, lost my shoes in Leningrad, and many more adventures that could never be predicted.

I'm calling my book *The Accidental Adventuress: My Wacky Life as a Travel Writer*—a title that will no doubt be changed by a publisher, if any. If I learned anything from writing about travel it's that you never know what's coming next, but it's always fun.

— *Marda Burton*
   New Orleans, Louisiana

Of Sheep and Specialization

I began to feel woozy as I watched the operation on an anesthetized pregnant sheep in a laboratory of the National Institutes of Health in Bethesda, Maryland. Here I was, on a science-writing fellowship that could give my career a big boost, and I absolutely could not faint. What a wimp these scientists would think me if I fell splat on the floor during this scientific procedure. Somehow I managed to keep myself upright as my head spun, although I turned my eyes away from the sheep's belly.

That was years ago, the sheep and her offspring are probably dead, and I've never regretted my decision to specialize in science and medicine. Although I have wide interests and am a feature writer at heart, writing about everything from coronary bypass surgery to mammography to health care reform to ovarian cancer to the high cost of new drugs and devices to nanotechnology to medical errors has been intellectually stimulating and richly rewarding. For balance, I developed a second specialty, spiritual/inspirational writing. These two specialties moved along on separate railroad tracks for quite awhile, and I jumped schizophrenically from one to the other. Now, happily, body and soul are increasingly connected in the eyes of scientists and doctors, and I can pursue my two specialties as a whole self.

— *Peggy Eastman*
Chevy Chase, Maryland

When I worked in offices, I thrived as the social center. I knew all the gossip, initiated the holiday toy drive and remembered birthdays. While I always worked hard, coworkers and I spent a lot of time in each other's offices.

Almost immediately after I started freelancing full-time in 2004, I was blindsided by the loneliness. My work plate was full, my husband sometimes worked at home and I enjoyed the flexibility. Still, freelancing was no match for the rich social life I had left.

So I sent an email to some local women writers, many of whom I vaguely knew. I told them I craved a group with whom to discuss best practices, vent and share some sisterly camaraderie. Would they be interested?

A week later, five of us of varying ages and experience levels met at a local coffeehouse. We laughed, lamented, encouraged. It was everything I missed.

Today, we have grown to about 25. Not everyone comes to our every-other-Friday gatherings. But our email listserv is strong—we ask questions, share resources and jobs, and send jokes. And the "regulars" who meet have become treasured friends.

As a freelancer, I may spend more time in my own office. But I am at peace knowing my coworkers are just a Friday morning away.

— *Melanie Lasoff Levs*
Atlanta, Georgia

Three hours into what turned out to be a six-hour interview with Pete Seeger, I was just getting around to asking what inspired him to write certain songs. To prompt him, I started singing "Where Have All the Flowers Gone," and, in his wavering 83 year old voice, Seeger began to sing along. I had goose bumps—realizing that although millions of people have sung this song over the years, and possibly tens of thousands have sung it along with him at concerts, I was having a nearly singular experience; singing Where Have All the Flowers Gone with the man who wrote it—just the two of us around his kitchen table. Being a writer allows me the privilege to have experiences I wouldn't ordinarily have, meet people I wouldn't, in "real life" have the chance to meet, and delve wholeheartedly into strange, complex, and foreign worlds all in the service of enlightening a wider audience. I love the fact that no two days are alike. On Monday, I could share a cup of coffee with a Holocaust survivor, on Thursday, catch a busy Bobby Kennedy, Jr. on the fly, and on Saturday write my impressions about an awesome tuna-tartar dish while chatting up the hot new chef. Being a writer allows me to live my own fantasy life!

— *Malerie Yolen-Cohen*
  Stamford, Connecticut

The Slings & Arrows of Rejection

I meet them every time I attend a cocktail party or business function—the stressed-out professionals who'd love to quit their jobs and try "something more fun." Like getting published.

I was cornered by one of these aspiring authors at a seminar recently—a man who works for a high-profile architecture firm but would rather be writing. He'd published essays in the local paper and wanted to publish more. But after receiving several rejection letters, he was ready to give up.

"How do you handle the rejection? he asked.

"The same way architects do when their building designs are rejected," I told him.

"Oh, no," he shot back. "That's not as personal."

Rejection and its evil twin, Criticism, are part of the writing life. Both keep in touch with me periodically, too. But another writer offered this consolation: If you're not getting rejection slips, you're not aiming high enough or sending out enough material.

As I reminded the guy from the architecture firm, rejection is hardly the sole province of publishing. Anything you dearly hope to achieve, including love itself, holds the possibility of loss.

It helps to remember that the craft of writing offers second chances. As Frank Lloyd Wright said, "A doctor can bury his mistakes, but an architect can only advise his client to plant vines." Thankfully, redemption is so much easier for writers. We can reorganize, revise, and send our stuff out again.

And the small victories are sweet. Not long ago, a favorite piece was rejected by a regional magazine. I tried again, and it was snapped up by a national publication for more money than I'd expected—and I hadn't changed a word. That doesn't happen as often as I'd like. Just often enough to fuel my hopes and make my work more fun than architecture.

— *Cindy La Ferle*
Royal Oak, Michigan

Writer With Baby

Having a baby alone at age 39 would be simple. I imagined her nursing for twenty minutes a couple times a day, and staying quietly in her crib the rest of the time while I researched and wrote my Los Angeles Weekly health column.

I named her Natanya (Gift from God in Hebrew). The child was on a schedule from the start: On the left, on the right, on the left, on the right. I was sure by the end of the first week that she would walk down the aisle at her high school graduation and stop for a nip at my breast en route to her diploma.

So Natanya and I were inseparable. I sat as far away from the nonionizing radiation of my Tandy Radio Shack computer (no mouse, and eight inch discs) as I could reach with my daughter in my lap, typing one handed. It was OK, I have unusually long arms.

We went to "Writing the Corporate A/V Script," a seminar by Stephen Poe for members of the Independent Writers of Southern California on February 22, 1986. Natanya was exactly three weeks old and full of interesting tricks. Do you know how loud a three week old can smack her lips when nursing or grunt when having a bowel movement? All fifty people in the room can tell you.

So Natanya and I more carefully chose our outings. It was OK. I could read Poe's 1.25 inch manual at home.

Writers find a way.

— *Carolyn Reuben*
   Sacramento, California

Why Freelance Writers Are Like White Blood Cells

The police and journalists have a traditional love-hate relationship. I think that's because the jobs are so much alike. We both do research. We work wherever the job takes us, and talk to whomever has information, be that the governor or the drug addict in the ghetto gutter. Other people go to their 9-5 daily jobs and sit in the same chair and do the same things and get out of the office for lunch. We spend the day roaming our "turf" and writing about it. Like the white blood cells that can squeeze through the spaces between other body cells as they make their rounds, we squeeze through the cracks in our society, seeking out the interesting to write about.

It's this daily difference, this endless variety, this peek into other lives and inside the daily news, that keeps us so fascinated by this job that we writers say we never retire; we just make that final deadline.

— *Steve Morrill*
   Tampa, Florida

Sometimes, my boss is a real pain in the rear. My boss is seriously moody, loving my work one minute, hating it the next. My boss gives me too many assignments at once, and then over-compensates by giving me too few. My boss ignores the vacation time I mapped out weeks ago because there was some big project she just couldn't turn down. My boss underpays and under-appreciates me. My boss is a stickler for perfection, won't cut me any slack, and expects me to be a Jill-of-all-trades: marketing guru, payroll officer, accountant, secretary, beat reporter, fact checker, transcriptionist, professional organizer (which I am definitely not), and more. Oh yeah, and of course, brilliant writer. My boss... is me.

— *Alison Fromme*
   Berkeley, California

By Me

A h, the byline, that double-edged sword. How remarkable it looks when it first appears on the page, your name suddenly transformed into a literary event. The name is you and you are it, but it is also more than you, it represents all the words and thoughts that you have shaped into a published article. You have worked for that byline and you deserve it. You sit back and bask in your fleeting hours of fame, for tomorrow that newspaper will be trash.

The phone rings off the hook as acquaintances call to say they read your article. You can't wait to publish the next one, and the one after that. You have a public, isn't it fun? Until one day you look at an article in disbelief. You didn't write that! An editor changed your words, changed your meaning, but your byline is still there. Or you were so sure you knew who paired up with Rodgers before Hammerstein that you didn't double-check the name. "Moss Hart" is published under your byline, but the correct name was Lorenz Hart, and your cheeks flame when a caller points out your error.

Or you might have dictated your story, saying: "The affable conductor juggles all of these activities effortlessly." But the transcriber misunderstands, and "effortlessly" is published as "fruitlessly." The conductor calls to complain, no longer so affable.

Now, after thousands of published articles and bylines, you hold your breath when the phone rings. You listen to the positive comments. And you wait for the dreaded, "but there was one mistake."

— *Roberta Hershenson*
New York, New York

"'The' ... Give Me A Dollar!"

True, in college I had a friend who wrote articles about the sex appeal of multicolored toenails for *Seventeen*, but it never really occurred to me that you could make a living as a writer. In my family a living meant a job with fixed hours, an employer, and sick days. Abby typed furiously at her MacClassic in her pajamas; I grew up believing having a real job meant wearing clothes to work.

After the birth of my second daughter, raiment was the least of my concerns. I had a toddler and a newborn and suddenly the working world was the last place I wanted to be, despite a hard-earned Ph.D. and many job offers (including one tenure track position) after grad school. When Athena was a few months old I wrote to magazines for submission guidelines and discovered the starting rate was a dollar a word. A dollar a word?! It was unthinkable. "'The' … Give me a dollar!" I cried to my husband, laughing so hard the baby giggled too. "'The cat,' …Give me two dollars!" The idea of being paid so much to write was as sweet as maple sugar.

Piles of rejections and some kill fees (ouch) later, I have published four books, written hundreds of newspaper and magazine articles, and I support our family of five through my writing. I usually get dressed before I start working. Today's task is the outline for an article for Smithsonian on the last herd of West African giraffes.

— *Jennifer Margulis*
Ashland, Oregon

When I tell people I'm a writer, they often treat me as though I said, "I'm unemployed," or ask my favorite question—"Are you a real writer?" I'm not sure what to say to that because the phrase means something different to nearly everyone who asks. People mean any of the following: being famous, writing fiction, starving for my art, making a living from fiction, making a living from any writing, or having a "real job" but publishing a poem now and then. Am I a real writer? I exist. That's a start. I write. Some weeks I don't feel like a real writer because I spend more time marketing and taking care of business than writing, but I do write for my living, and I write for pleasure. My mother and father write, so I even have the writer gene. I realize now that part of the freelance writing job is answering a lot of questions: Yes, I suppose I'm a real writer. Yes, I live in poverty, but I'm sure it's temporary. Yes, I have written published books—seven of them. No, I'm not unemployed; I'm self employed. Yes, I'm sure your life story is fascinating. No, I'm sorry; I don't have time to write it. Yes, It's hard. Yes, It's worth it. Yet I do think it would be easier sometimes to spin a little fiction and say I'm a dental assistant.

— *Linda Eve Diamond*
  Dania, Florida

What Do I Know?

There are few things more pleasing than discovering the expression of a thought that has been lurking in the back of your mind for years or decades, but has never quite come into focus. Margaret Attwood provided me with this pleasure in the following quotation.

"Everyone thinks writers must know more about the inside of the human head, but that is wrong. They know less. That's why they write. Trying to find out what everyone else takes for granted."

These few words lit up a dark corner that has been nagging at me since I was about twenty years old.

"Why do we write?"

There are lots of plausible answers to the question: I've used most of them in my lifetime. But, as Attwood implies, the real reason I write is that we don't understand anything about other human beings, and we are trying to find out.

This explanation works for me. The human world is awash with enthusiasms and manias, most of which are incomprehensible to me: sports, religion, and war are three of the big ones. I just can't understand what anybody sees in any of them, yet they seem to be as essential to human happiness as food or sex.

It's disappointing that forty years or more of writing haven't brought me any closer to answers, but at least I tried. In the end, I'm happy to relax into the bemused acquiescence of the great French essayist Michel de Montaigne. In middle age he became skeptical about the possibility of any true knowledge, and adopted the motto: "Que sais-je?" – What do I know?

— *David Bouchier*
Stony Brook, New York

Illusion of Isolation

Like Trigorin in Chekhov's "The Sea Gull," many writers I know would like to have a water-side retreat on a lake or a river or by the sea, a place to recharge batteries far removed from madding crowds. I am one of the lucky ones. I have just such a place: a loft-study in a summer house on an island off Wellfleet on Cape Cod. The house, named by my Dutch wife, is called "Nooitgedagt," meaning, in colloquial English, "Who'd a thunk it!"

During long winter days and nights, whether at home or far away, I often spend hours ruminating about that peaceful Shangri-La, which, like the cathedral at Ste. Michelle, can be reached only by crossing a causeway at low tide. I think about my study, the piles of books and papers, the computer on the desk, and the 180 degree water view out the windows.

Sometimes we go there in winter, a challenge for it is not always possible to cross to the island owing to ice floes that settle on the road left by ebbing tides. When spring arrives, I inevitably take a quick trip to the Cape. Ostensibly it is to check on the house but actually it is because I long to sit in my study and pretend it is already summer. Then, sometime in June, like the migrating birds that nest on the beaches and in the marshes, we move out to Nooitgedagt and settle in for another season of reading and writing—and, like Trigorin, anguishing about what is going on in the real world from which I was so eager to escape.

— *Peter I. Rose*
Northampton, Massachusetts

Freelancing Life

I once wrote an article about the influx of profit-making educational companies. In that article, a representative at a teacher's union said teachers choose their calling because they love educating kids and don't dream about owning a Rolex. I thought that a perfect metaphor for becoming a freelancer. No one chooses this pursuit with all of its vagaries and uncertainties to get rich, but the rewards transcend dollar and cents.

Becoming a freelance writer results in following Thoreau's advice in *Walden*, "I wanted to live deep and suck all the marrow out of life."

In my 20-plus years of freelancing, I have tried hard to become the quintessential generalist. I've written about the arts, tennis, restaurants, small business, education, investments and high-tech.

I've spent a day with Eddie Murphy, interviewed Mel Gibson on a set in Kingsport, Tennessee, and questioned Fred D. Thompson of "Law & Order" and short-lived presidential aspirations on how an attorney could turn into an actor. I've been accosted by a Unitarian Church member when spending a day with a process-server and visited the bowels of Chinatown's eateries with a New York City health inspector. I profiled a communications professor who had been quoted by major publications 522 times in two years, described the mayor of Pittsburgh's plan for creating new jobs to replace the fading steel industry, and interviewed the restaurant critics of *The New York Times*, *The Washington Post*, and *USA Today* on how they do their job.

I'm still wearing the same $50 watch I bought 10 years ago, but my experiences as a freelance writer have enriched my life far beyond the worth of a Rolex.

— *Gary M. Stern*
 New York, New York

My writing career spans living in New York City and now in Los Angeles. I'm a fickle writer. I'm not loyal to any particular genre. It's the eclectic-ness of my writing that keeps me intrigued, challenged, and stimulated. While living in New York City, I wrote sexual how-to articles from a woman's point of view for men's magazines and also problem/resolution fiction stories for women's confession story magazines. When I moved to Los Angeles, (after having married Eddie, the man I love), I wrote sensual romance novels in which the hero and heroine have intensely emotional conflicts that keep them apart, but in the end, their love surpasses all. (I'm a total romantic.) I've worked as a full-time writer and also a part-time writer/part-time medical editor working for various orthopedic surgeons, depending on how financially secure I want to feel. My work has been rejected by some of the top magazine and book editors, the letters of which I keep as shiny trophies in my file drawer to show how hard I've worked and never given up. Writing is part of my DNA. I will keep writing until the day I'm lying with hands folded at my chest in a satin-covered coffin. Hmmm... knowing myself, while lying there with nothing to do (I'm not a time waster), I'll probably be conjuring up an exciting new book idea I hope will sell in the next lifetime!

— *Patty Salier*
  Los Angeles, California

The Writing Life

In my mid-thirties, I worked as a feature writer and editor at the *Daily Progress* in Charlottesville, Virginia where a fellow reporter dubbed me "the death and disease editor." I wrote on a variety of topics but did pursue more stories than most with doctors and psychiatrists. It seemed I was interested in their medical expertise and strategies for survival.

Some years later as a freelance writer, I again pursued topics on medicine, health and healing. I discovered that having a particular focus was a plus in pitching ideas to magazines; it also gave me endless questions I wanted to explore.

In 2000, my father died at the age of 90. Although he lived a long, good life, when his years ended, even 90 felt too few. A writer apparently still on the "death and disease'" beat, I went back to the experts for answers on aging and survival. I sought the guidance of elders whom I admired for their continuing vitality and creativity. I talked with older friends and acquaintances and well known men and women, all still working at what they loved. I found Walter Cronkite still publishing his opinions, Carol Channing still singing and dancing. Such mentors answered my questions, offering me comfort, counsel and wise steps to follow. In the end, writing a book about my father and those still so strongly engaged in life, became its own vital tool for survival.

— *Ellizabeth Meade Howard*
  Charlottesville, Virginia

Rejoicing in a Career About Words

As writers we sometimes grumble about the loneliness of what we do. Being underpaid. Coping with rejection. Realistic complaints, all. Yet I feel so blessed to be in this profession, to be in a position to add value and encouragement to peoples' lives.

Words can work wonders. For me they led to a mini-empire of writing, speaking, and consulting. This three-legged stool provides a sound foundation for an author bitten fiercely by the entrepreneurial bug. In addition to selling rights to my work and/or receiving self-publishing revenue, I forged and sold two thriving book shepherding businesses.

Perhaps sweetest of all are the friendships I have with people around the world, many of whom I've never met face to face. Yet we exchange Christmas cards and they drop me a grateful or uplifting email from time to time. Where else, but from the written word, would such loving fans emerge?

And in preparation for writing travel pieces, I've had the privilege of delving into behind-the-scenes secrets and experiences few are ever privy to. Plus being a writer sometimes gives you an interview opportunity to meet and talk with a celebrity or CEO few can access. Ah, the writing life—where the wonder of words can open lucrative, exciting, and magical doors.

— *Marilyn Ross*
  Buena Vista, Colorado

Writing Bareback

"STOP!" I wail. "STOP TALKING! ALL OF YOU!" In an attempt to gain control, I lift my blazing fingers from the keyboard, lace them in my lap, draw a deep cleansing breath. The sudden and blissful silence is remarkable. Their obedience stuns me.

Scares me.

What if they never speak again?

"I need you to take turns," I say in a polite whisper. "How do you expect me to meet my deadline when you're all moving and yammering at once?" I close my eyes to eradicate the sight of the blink-blinking cursor. I need to see them.

Only the spooky whites of their blink-blinking eyes surround me. They're sneaking toward me from the distant future, creeping up on me from the past. I feel their breath rustling my hair, chilling my backbone, gusting up my nostrils as they fill me, haunt me, own me, overpower me with their aliveness and will.

Yes!

But I need cooperation here, especially from Acting Mayor Gladys McKern who is, as usual, going nose-to-nose with me. "Gladys," I say, "how would you like it if I mistakenly wrote that you flipped bacon at Harry's Grill?" She pins me to my chair with that threatening stare of hers.

I open my eyes, blink her away, my fingertips daring to once again land on the keyboard. In seconds they're click-clicking as fast as they can to keep up with the movie that, at least for now, gratefully runs in my head, one scene at a time.

— *Charlene Ann Baumbich*
   Glen Ellyn, Illinois

Postscripts

"Have you considered writing as a career?" The question appeared at the top of my term paper in a long-ago English class.

Actually, I hadn't. In mid-twentieth century Detroit, teenage girls aspired to a career as secretary at Ford Motor Company. But a series of scholarships opened other doors. By the time I left Michigan for California with my new husband, I packed a Master's Degree in German together with my bridal gown.

A stint as elementary school teacher in Long Beach lasted until the arrival of our own offspring in the 1960s. Then I resumed teaching in the burgeoning field of ESL—a move that prompted the study of Spanish and subsequent involvement in Bilingual Education.

With early retirement in 1986, I announced my intention of parlaying my language skills into a career as travel writer. "That's nice, Dear," said my husband.

Of course, I suffered the slings and arrows of any new freelance writer—rejection, low pay, fierce competition—along with the humbling realization that marketing skills carry as much weight as good writing. Many of my early articles were accounts of my sojourns at language schools in France, Italy, and especially Mexico.

Eventually, writing assignments and wanderlust led to more exotic destinations, from Easter Island to Kathmandu. When the list came out recently of the "new" Seven Wonders of the World, each one evoked vivid personal memories.

Writing as a career? Yes, I've considered it. For me, the financial rewards are secondary; the experience, priceless.

— *Joyce Gregory Wyels*
  Los Alamitos, California

The Writers' Family

H anging out with other writers is what keeps me sane.
After attending an all-day writing workshop, I later mused that being with fellow writers is sort of like going to a family reunion. Even though it's a motley group and you all have that weird cowlick, you share the same family line and a sense of belonging in the comfortable company of each other's weirdness.

Writing kinfolk also inherently understand the hazards of this particular profession. Rejection. Discouragement. Deadlines. Financial pressures. For every blessed stretch of brilliant and prolific writing we might enjoy, we also battle daily distractions and the will to stay disciplined. There are readers who revere our words in all their glorious perfection, and others who approach our manuscripts with a sharpened red pencil. A sculptor needn't worry that a critic will come along and chisel off a chunk of her masterpiece, and a painter rarely encounters a brush-wielding editor who moves his figures around and asks him to repaint the background. If you're a writer, however, people will inevitably mess with your work.

We're constantly urged to build our 'platforms,' be visible, get out there and promote ourselves, when what most of us would really rather do is just write. Outsiders don't understand, but writers do; when we gather together, we're bound not only by the peculiarities of what we do but also by the price we've paid to be in the family—cowlicks and all.

— *Eliza Cross*
Centennial, Colorado

I come from a family of freelancers, a father who made award-winning films, a stepmother writing for television and a mother whose magazine assignments ranged from car races in Florida to the Chicago Eight trial. For a young girl growing up in Toronto, Canada's media capital, driving every teacher mad with my constant refrain of "Why?"— a habit that later proved handy—journalism was always my only choice.

By the time I graduated college, I'd been writing freelance for half a dozen national publications. While my formal education taught me to read Chaucer in Middle English, I'd begun to amass the arcana that comes from life as a generalist, work I continue today. I'd already learned how Adidas got their name, (Adi Dassler, the man who created them), how radium decays to radon gas, what a parachutist's face looks like before she leaps from an airplane wing.

I've also since worked at three major dailies, including the *New York Daily News*, and my freelancing background means I never run out of ideas—as we all know, no ideas means no income!

I've interviewed convicted felons, elected officials, Olympic athletes, FBI agents and Boy Scouts; I especially value the intellectual fearlessness this work demands.

I still love writing, but I've come to hate the pay. Stagnant rates make producing thoughtful, quality journalism for a living hard, non-stop work. I'm lobbying Apple for a new computer icon—beads of sweat!

— *Caitlin Kelly*
Tarrytown, New York

Ode to the Freelance Life

Freelancing's just another word
for "You don't have a job,"
or so I'm told by those who think
the life I lead is odd.
No pension plan, no IRAs,
no insurance, not one bit.
Not even any colleagues
to giggle at my wit.
A lonely life in many ways,
long days till the work is done,
and yet, and yet—the strangest thing—
this crazy life is fun.

I commute in purple flip-flops
turquoise robe and tangled hair,
because to reach my office
I just climb a flight of stairs.
There are no office meetings,
there's no water cooler chat,
no grouchy CEO or boss,
and I can live with that.
I work when the spirit moves me—
if it's 3 A.M., that's fine,
I'll get the work done, to be sure,
but in my own sweet time.

(continued on next page)

This is not a life for everyone—
paychecks come and go,
there are 15-hour workdays,
and others that are slow.
Most editors are friendly,
while others are plain rude—
One buys each golden word I write,
the next has attitude.
There are no perfect jobs of course,
but mine comes close, you see,
It's a joy to go to work each day
when the boss of me—is me.

— *Karen Hammond*
  South Bristol, Maine

🕯   🕯   🕯

A writer always hopes she reaches people, but I'm always so touched when I get concrete evidence of that. Twice now, two retirees have written to me—using typewriters—about an article I've written. They each lived alone, and to think that they actually took the time to write amazed me. I pictured them, sitting in their easy chair or at the kitchen table reading the paper, and then getting up and walking to the typewriter. They let me know I had made a connection. You better believe I answered each letter.

— *Pat Olsen*
  Tinton Falls, New York

The Philosophy of Me

I'm a writer because I write. I'm a freelancer because I like to be free. (I don't know where the "lancer" fits in.) Anyway, it's a no brainer why I've lasted 27 years as a self-employed writer of articles, books, and book reviews, with part-time editing work thrown in for good measure.

Even though I'm in the right profession, I sometimes stray. Right now I think I want to be an artist, having discovered talent in the areas of fine art photography and decoupage collage.

Even though I'm in the right profession, I sometimes dilly-dally with love. Right now it's with a muscle-bound commercial fisherman, who takes me out in his boat a lot.

Hey, I'm a writer but I have to have a life, don't I?

Actually, as any writer worth his sea salt knows, these dalliances serve to enrich my life and make me a better writer. There aren't many things I do that don't trigger the urge to "write about it." I've just handed in to a biology magazine a 3000-word piece on seaweed. (See paragraph 3.) I've got an outline planned for a book on decoupage and spirituality. And I already use my photographs to illustrate my articles and make them more saleable.

Did I mention that I'm in the "write" profession because it pays? If you think it doesn't pay enough, ask any starving artist—or even a fisherman, in these days of stringent regulations—what he or she earns.

I write, therefore I am able to do what I am—and pay the bills.

— *Loraine Page*
Wadling River, New York

My Most Unforgettable Sale

As a freelance sports writer, my "Mount Everest" was making it into *Sports Illustrated*. In the early '70s I racked up three straight sales to SI's nostalgia column, "Yesterday," and began to think of quitting my "day job" as an advertising account executive and going fulltime as a freelancer.

Then I got a rejection.

A few months later a Southern California airport van picked me up to take me to Detroit for indoctrination in my new "day job." A middle-aged couple who had attended a tennis camp at Coto de Caza was already on board. Our conversation turned to sports.

"I'm a freelance sports writer," I said to the man, "I've had articles in *Sports Illustrated*."

He smiled and said, "I'm Gilbert Rogin, Managing Editor of *Sports Illustrated*."

I wasted no time in telling Mr. Rogin how disappointed I was my last submission had been rejected. "What was it about?" he asked.

"The record for catching a baseball dropped from the highest altitude," I replied.

"Send it to me and I'll give it another look."

A couple weeks later, I came home from work and my wife was out of the house before I could park the car. "They're going to buy your story!'

I read the *Sports Illustrated* letter. They wanted to buy my idea, would pay full price but would rewrite it and run it with a staff writers' byline.

It was an agonizing decision. It took almost a full minute. There's one thing that beats a byline. Its spelled C-H-E-C-K.

— *Vince Agul*
Murrietra, California

My Place to Write Has Changed

The newsroom of *The Peru Daily Tribune* brimmed with activity especially near deadline. While it was over 30 years ago, I can still recall the tension-filled room with ringing phones and stacks of newsprint on various desks shoved right next to each other. In this pre-computer environment, when we needed to write, each of us crawled into our private mental space and focused on telling our story. As a young intern reporter that summer in my hometown of Peru, Indiana, I was filled with learning and insight about my chosen field of journalism. After a story meeting around 7 a.m., I would work on my assigned story and pound out my copy before the 11 a.m. deadline, when I had to hand it to our city editor. About 3 p.m. my words appeared in the afternoon paper, which rolled off the presses located in the same building.

Today after writing for more than 50 magazines and pounding out more than 60 books with traditional publishers and reams of other printed material, my environment for writing has radically changed. Instead of a manual typewriter, I use a wireless computer keyboard; yet my excitement about writing and telling stories continues as strong as ever. Instead of a busy newsroom, I work in my quiet home office. Like years ago, my continual thirst for new insight continues unabated. A key part of my education and learning as a writer has been my association with the ASJA and each of you. Thank you.

— *W. Terry Whalin*
Scottsdale, Arizona

My Life as a Travel Writer

Under the fluorescent lights of a windowless, community center classroom, six people looked at me expectantly. My first students. I had three hours a night for eight weeks to "introduce them to travel writing."

"Why are you here?" I asked.

"I love traveling and I love writing," most of them said. But though some of them had backpacked for a year at a time, most of their writing had been confined to e-mails to friends - e-mails which, so several of them told me, had been greeted with rapturous cries for "More!"

They wondered if travel writing could become their profession, or at least, an income-producing part of their lives.

I don't recall if I gave them the bad news right away or if I held off for a week or two.

I've made most of my living as a writer and editor for more than 40 years. Fifteen of those years were in corporate staff positions. The rest of the time, I've been a freelancer.

There were a few heady years when I earned $100,000 or more. That's when I was doing a lot of corporate work - brochures, newsletters, video scripts, white papers and so on. But in 1994, I discovered travel writing, and like kudzu, it quickly took over. My income plummeted.

"Being a travel writer is a great way to live but a lousy way to make a living," I told my students. The pay is low and print markets that used to be decent have been drying up because of competition from Internet sites that pay contributors little or nothing.

But, alas, there's nothing I want to do more than be a travel writer. To me, it's an exhilarating form of life-long learning.

At the end of the class, my students turned in their evaluations. One of them, the best writer in the class, whose work was definitely publishable, said, "I learned what I needed to know." Last I heard, she was thinking of going back to being a high school teacher. That would, at least, give her summers off and time to travel.

— *Terese Loeb Kreuzer*
New York, New York

The Miracle of Creativity

Artists and writers of all types gifted with creativity frequently have extended lives, remain in good health to the end, and experience a sense of fulfillment.

According to the great writer Anatole Broyard, the artist has an antibody against illness and pain. In the depth of his Parkinson's Disease, all Broyard's old, trivial selves dissolved and he was reduced to his essence. Wilem de Kooning at ninety-three years of age was virtually immobilized by Alzheimer's disease. With the support of Elaine de Kooning, he began a new style of painting.

Georgia O'Keeffe has been a major figure in American art since the 1920s. Although her eyesight was eroded by macular degeneration, she worked unassisted until 1984, to the advanced age of 96. She died on March 6, 1986 at the age of 98.

Linda Hargrove, the Original Blue Jean Country Queen, was diagnosed with leukemia in 1986. Her career took a drastic turn downward and was literally "put on hold." She was given the prognosis of death within 6 years. Recovered and cancer-free, she resurrected her career and released a new CD.

I have always felt that creativity and the source of life are of a piece, and that when we are able to understand one we will also understand the other. The other day, my granddaughters and I were working on a few pieces of sculpture. When we finished, there stood a little man and his dog, looking as alive as we did. It was uncanny. Out of nothing, an inert lump of clay, there now was something. It reminded me of the feeling I had on first seeing my son Zane as a newborn infant. There was nothing there, and then all of a sudden, there was a person.

— *Alma Bond*
  New York, New York

I don't have a mechanical bone in my body. If the machine has an on/off switch, I can make it work. Beyond that, I become easily flustered. Years ago, when I taught school, I gave up being the all-knowing instructor figure and sought out the nearest geek (a term that hadn't yet been invented, but we still recognized the type) to run the projector and other equipment—under the guise of being teacher's helper.

So, it's amazing that now my days are spent in front of a computer clicking on words and tabs and drop-down menus, always expecting each command to be obeyed explicitly. To me it's pure magic; I have only the foggiest notion of what's happening inside this complex machine. And I really don't want to know—until it revolts. Or I need to update my web site. Or write a blog. Or send a huge photo file.

Terror knots my belly each time I click an unknown icon. Will it make matters worse instead of better? I watch the computer flick images in rapid sequence, loving and hating it at the same time. But it's my lifeline now, and the struggle continues daily for peaceful coexistence.

Is there a shrink for machine-phobic writers? Or an instructor for unblocking closed minds? Maybe I just need to accept my limitations, do what I can, and kick pride out of the way. Hey, kids, how about a little help for Mom?

— *Beverly Burmeier*
  Austin, Texas

If I didn't become a writer, I'd fling big words around at each opportunity of correspondence like a pompous ass, boring my unwitting victims beyond the point of apology.

I've had all kinds of jobs. But I've always had the most fun—and felt most honest—interviewing this band, or writing that radio spot. So I got the hint and went whole hog. Life has shown me that in order to earn a living, I have no choice but to power on, fuel up, and enter a vacuous state of inertia—ironic as that is.

Another indubitable irony of this profession is that nothing is "free." There are still deadlines and schedules imposed by paycheck-signing figures of superiority that loom overhead—albeit figuratively—judging the quality and integrity of your output at every turn. And you are charged with putting on their voice of choice and stepping lively to that day's choreographed routine. Your job is to solve their problems, while simultaneously struggling to filter through a modicum of your own little something. And in your nonexistent spare time, you must find a way to perform as account strategist and accounts payable department. It's a hell of a lot of work.

So what's the outstanding benefit of this path? If you're really lucky, you might just write something that someone can relate to. And you sometimes get to do it in your pajamas. I really like to work in my pajamas.

— *Vivian Manning*
   Brooklyn, New York

Being a travel writer is like being a Boy Scout: it's essential to be prepared for anything, but better to be prepared for *everything*.

I am living proof that Mother Nature often presents a myriad of problems:

•1977 – The first snow in the history of the Bahamas occurred while I was hosting a press trip at Princess Hotels, the client I represented for M. Silver Associates PR.

•1979 – No matter what island I tried, it rained for virtually all of a 10-day February trip to Hawaii, where I was sent to scout a tour for American Express.

•1992 – The worst earthquake in the world that year occurred at 5:04 a.m. on June 28, a Sunday morning, while I was on the 22nd floor of a Los Angeles hotel on the second day of an eight-day California assignment.

•1996 – Kansas City had its only tornado of the year while I was in town covering the Society for American Baseball Research convention.

•1997 – A day after covering the All-Star Game, a 59-minute flight from Cleveland to Newark became a 13-hour odyssey because of a squall line that wouldn't quit..

During other writing road trips, I've experienced the worst flood in the history of Catalina, a *desert* island; an equally-unlikely four-hour fog delay at Phoenix airport; frigid March weather in Orlando; and a Cape Hatteras gale on the QE2.

I wonder what Oklahoma City has in store during the national conference of the North American Travel Journalists Association from June 24-27, 2008. As founder and president of the group, I'll be there—with one eye on the sky.

— *Dan Schlossberg*
   Fair Lawn, New Jersey

To Bill...or Not to Bill

About six months into my first year as a freelance copywriter, I was sitting at my gynecologist's office waiting...and waiting...and waiting. It's always irritating to cool your heels in a doctor's office, but now, as an entrepreneur who billed on an hourly basis, this dead time was costing me money. As the minutes ticked by, I did a slow-burn, calculating the lost wages at $75 an hour. As someone new to the world of freelancing and anxious about not receiving a regular paycheck, I was a clock watcher for the better part of a year.

Now, in my eighth year of successful freelance copywriting and feature writing, I've taken a more relaxed approach to billable and non-billable hours.

I'm not a junior attorney or advertising executive who has to account every hour of every week to a tyrannical boss or risk losing her job. My schedule, like that of most creative professionals, is fluid. Much of what I regularly do—reading, researching, pitching, networking, daydreaming—is, in fact, unbillable. To keep my creative juices flowing, I routinely block out time to recharge by traveling, visiting museums, hitting the gym, seeing first-run movies, lunching with friends, having a massage.

The result is that some weeks I don't bill a full 40 hours. But I've learned that's okay. I still get impatient, but now I can stop fretting while I'm in my dentist's waiting room. And who knows? I might even brainstorm a lucrative query while reading the latest issue of *People*.

— *Suzanne Wright*
   Atlanta, Georgia

Why I Write

There ought to be compelling reasons why someone would choose to spend a life cooped up in isolation before a computer screen while others are outside "playing."

I'll be honest about mine. Writing fits my personality. Although at times I can speak articulately, generally I am not very good on my feet. In a cruel quirk of timing, my brain always seems to come up with the pithy retort, the spontaneous joke or the brilliant observation a second or two too late, when the moment has passed, causing me to swallow my words. Or it comes up with nothing at all. This may be an outgrowth of my diffident nature, which deters me from expressing myself brazenly the way others do. Perhaps I'm a coward at heart, at least when it comes to the spoken word.

No so with writing. Given time to think about what I want to say, emboldened by the sheer power of words when artfully assembled, I view writing as an all-purpose tool—indeed, sometimes a weapon—for achieving various objectives. As an advertising copywriter I resort to all sorts of verbal antics to wheedle money out of people (in an effort to earn some). As an author and essayist, it's the altering of behaviors and beliefs I'm after (okay, and the money, too).

Regardless, armed with the ability to launch long- and short-range verbal missiles at virtually any target I choose with near anonymous impunity, both the process and the anticipated results become enormously fun for me.

And that's why I write.

— *G. Gaynor McTigue*
Fairfield, Connecticut

In the final analysis, a writing career depends on one's personal goals as they emerge and evolve in a lifetime. When I was a teenager in the mid-1930s, I found inspiration in the work of Sinclair Lewis. He showed America the truth about itself. In 1926, when he declined the Pulitzer Prize, Lewis said, "Every compulsion is put upon writers to become safe, polite, obedient, and sterile." Like Lewis, I did not want to be safe, sterile or sorry.

It isn't about money. Yes, money matters, but I think the challenge is to write something of meaning, beyond the moment, and of self-fulfillment. In my writing career, I came to believe society needs transformation, a viewpoint of human concern to counter the greed and deceit so transparent in this business today. And I have tried to act on that belief.

The older I grew, the more I loved my work and the subjects I wrote about; I found pleasure in digging deeper and in learning through research and reading, and in working with editors, who almost always wanted only that I improve my writing and that it come through as mine and written from the heart.

I find quotable passages where I least expect them, as in Thomas Merton's *Raids on the Unspeakable*. "News," he wrote, "becomes merely a new noise in the mind, briefly replacing the noise that went before it and yielding to the noise that comes after it, so that eventually everything blends into the same monotonous and meaningless rumor. News? There is so much news that there is no room left for the true tidings, the Good News, The Great Joy."

I like to think that in my time and my own way I endeavored to spread The Great Joy—to illuminate the human condition by refusing to put a price tag on the priceless."

— *Michael Frome*
  Port Washington, Wisconsin

I love to write and I still marvel that I can earn money doing it. The work in writing for me isn't in the writing, it's in brevity. With most assignments I find myself cutting, chopping, hacking and deleting the words I work so hard to put together. Realizing this time suck was also siphoning money from my pay rate, I opted to swap my usual New Year's resolution (to floss every day, it was hopeless anyway) with this: write within the boundary of my assigned word count. Genius! In order to keep a 2500-word feature from growing into 15,000 words (seriously, this has happened) I must have a plan; I must be deliberate; and as suggested by some colleagues, I must leave some rocks unturned. My first assignment for the year was a series of short profiles, which I happily agreed to write. These would be a breeze, my editor promised, only 150 words. What? As in 1-5-0? Are we missing a zero? That "easy" little assignment nearly drove me insane. I failed miserably at a 150-word first draft and my New Year's resolution. But, like any exercise, the process was good for me. If not for assigned word counts I would go on beyond necessity, like I do on most answering machines. I need to learn to say good bye before the beep. Which, my dear friends, is coming soon. (I'm going to deliver no more than 250 words, as required for this story.)

— *Kara Douglass Thom*
  Savage, Minnesota

Writing: My Lifeline

When I was told eight years ago this month that I had needed immediate brain surgery to remove a life-threatening brain tumor called a meningioma, my greatest fear wasn't shaving my head or taking medication for the rest of my life. Rather it was what would happen if my neurosurgeon accidentally scraped off one too many neurons or tampered with the part of my brain that gave me the ability to write, be creative, and be me.

Despite months of struggling with words as my probed gray squishy gray matter slowly regained its shape, I finally managed to learn all over again how to coherently commit scattered thoughts to paper. That's all I've ever known how to do.

Whether it's been interviewing the president of J. Crew during a college internship at a start up business magazine, making the cover story of *Baseball Weekly* for a piece on dispelling the myths of baseball wives or finally becoming a published author before my 40th birthday, writing has always been and will always be my lifeline.

Writing hasn't given me six figures, fame or landed me on the *NYT's* best-seller list, but it has given me the courage to accept rejection, taught me that eventually a slammed door has to open and how to be a voice for those who don't have one.

It's allowed me to be creative, which is exactly what I am.

— *Liz Holzemer*
Highlands Ranch, Colorado

Doing the Editor Dance

The most frustrating thing about writing is all the factors involved in getting a book deal that have nothing to do with the quality of my work. Often editors have tunnel vision about what's needed for a book to sell—pressure from other editors to sign authors with this or that—or they jump to conclusions without reading the whole proposal.

I've done over 300 radio and TV interviews, including *Oprah*, and have been quoted in dozens of publications. Yet my platform has often been deemed not strong enough. Sometimes I want to scream, "What must I do to please you? Run naked to get your attention?" Now that my platform is finally acceptable, they want to know how often I speak, and they continue to find new and improved problems. Yet my sales figures are good.

Living according to my "rule of ONE" keeps me grounded. I only need to connect with ONE person who's right for me. This mindset has worked for meeting a romantic partner, and I remind musicians they only need ONE record label, manager, etc., to recognize their talents. Those who aren't right don't matter. What counts is the ONE who says "yes," not those who say "no." I recall this when dancing to whims of book editors and focus on attracting the one right ONE to sign me.

I look forward to reaching a point where my profile is so strong that getting contracts for new titles won't be the issue, but instead, it will be how big my advance is!

— *Daylle Deanna Schwartz*
New York, New York

I have been a writer since second grade. (I waited a year to get the whole printing thing down pat). Most of the time I love being a writer—the creativeness of it, the satisfaction of communicating thoughts and ideas to readers I'll never see and never know but trust are out there somewhere reading what I wrote, the undeniable sense that this is what I was meant to do. While I can (and have) done other things, writing is the big "it" for me.

That's most of the time. Then there are those days (or weeks or months) when the writing gene takes a left turn and goes somewhere else—anywhere except this 10-by-12 room where I do most of my work. Oh, it leaves a few stray relatives hanging around, just enough to get the magazine articles or corporate projects completed. But the real writing— the fiction and essays I do for me first (and then the rest of the world second)—well, that hangs out in cold storage somewhere until the gene comes back and defrosts it.

I hate those days (or weeks or months). I hate wondering why I ever thought I could be a writer and fearing that the last truly creative thing I wrote is in fact the last truly creative thing I will ever write. I hate the whole fear/self-doubt/uncertainty that comes with the package.

But I don't hate it enough to give it up. So I guess I will just keep on being a writer.

— *Nancy Christie*
  Austintown, Ohio

Chapter 4
Telling Stories

Some writers never watch strangers reading their work. But if you're lucky, it will happen to you!

Early in my freelance writing career, I sold an article about ear-piercing to a local magazine. Along with practical information was a lively history of the 5,000 year old practice. "Ear rings" had been valued as protective charms against blindness since Biblical times, Egyptians pierced the ears of their sacred cats, and Julius Caesar, King Charles I, and William Shakespeare had worn earrings, too.

Soon after "A Piercing Look at Earrings" was published, I noticed a copy of the magazine in my dentist's waiting room. I also saw a patient who was restless and agitated. Checking the time on her watch and sighing repeatedly, she picked up and put down one magazine after another, until she selected "my" magazine. Still shifting impatiently in her seat, she flipped through the pages ... stopped ... and began to read. As casually as possible, I glanced over. What had captured her attention? My article.

I was tempted to tap her on the shoulder and boast, "Hey! That's my story! I wrote it!" but I already had all the satisfaction I needed. For the next few minutes, that patient was calm and relaxed because reading enabled her to escape, albeit briefly, from her impending woes. The experience had a magical effect on me, and it also gave me the confidence to start submitting my work to broader (and better paying) markets.

— *Susan J. Gordon*
  White Plains, New York

Best Payday of My Life

People say freelance writing doesn't pay all that well, which is often true if you're counting only money.

In 1980, for example, Doubleday published my first book, *Dancing without Music: Deafness in America*, about what I had learned, mostly at Gallaudet College (as it was then known), of the life, language and history of America's deaf community. An article had led to a book contract and a respectable, though hardly lavish, advance. Deafness and sign language were pretty exotic then, but it's not bragging to say that *Dancing* instantly became a classic in that small world, remaining in print continuously, except for six months in 1988, ever since. It has sold steadily, but never earned a lot.

Then, a few weeks ago, I was idly surfing Amazon.com—OK, I was enviously checking sales figures for some friends' recent books— when I looked up *Dancing*. There was a recent post by someone called Deafscribe.

"This book changed my life," his subject line read. Almost 30 years ago, he explained, he was a 19-year-old with a progressive hearing loss that would soon make him deaf, but he knew nothing about deafness. He discovered *Dancing* at the library, and, based on what he read, decided to go to Gallaudet. Arriving "as an immigrant," he found a warm welcome from the deaf community and a satisfying life within it for 25 years. "I shudder to think how different my life might be if I had not read this book," he wrote.

Talk about a million-dollar payday!

— *Beryl Lieff Benderly*
  Washington, D.C.

Easy Come, Hard Go

"Take it off," he said. The band played. I took it off.

"Take if off," he said again. The band played on. I took it off.

What was this, a tryout for a burlesque show? If so, what was I, a slightly softig, middle-aged mother of two grown sons, doing there?

"Can't wear them," said the TV producer, pointing to the bracelets on my wrist. "They'll clink and ruin the sound track."

Another lesson learned while promoting my Doubleday book, *A Woman's Book of Money.*

When I got home the phone rang as I opened the door.

"Is this Sylvia Auerbach?" a mellifluous male voice asked.

"It is," I said.

"THE Sylvia Auerbach who was interviewed on TV this morning?"

"The very one," I said, my heart beating a little faster.

"Great interview. That will get you on other shows. Are you interested?"

(Am I interested? Is Bill Gates rich?)

"Of course," I said. I threw back my shoulders while visions of TV contracts danced in my head.

"I represent the ZYX Group," Mr. Mellifluous said. "We recorded the show, and we think you should have the tape. "We'll be delighted to send it to you—for a small fee of $25."

I glared at the phone. My shoulders sagged.

"Thanks, but no thanks," I hissed.

I was tempted to utter a four-letter word, but I bit my tongue as I slammed down the receiver.

After all, there's always another time.

Like all ASJA writers, hope springs eternal.

— *Sylvia Auerbach*
Philadelphia, Pennsylvania

I pitched an article to an editor at a magazine and followed up for six months with no success. A year later (actually, 14 months later), the editor calls me up out of the blue and offers me an assignment. The assignment had nothing to do with the topic I had pitched, but had she kept my information on file and called me up when she needed me.

I was happy and accepted the assignment, but it also got me thinking. Between the pitch and the paycheck, I had over a year and a half to develop relationships with other, more responsive editors. I decided that I'd rather work with them. However, the experience taught me to never give up on a query.

— *Margarette Burnette*
  Woodstock, Georgia

Some years ago I learned of a screenwriter who pitched a treatment to a film producer. As the writer was leaving the office, he remembered he needed a copy of a document about an unrelated subject. He asked the producer's secretary if she would make a copy for him. "Of course," she said. "Follow me," She led him to the copier room. That was where he spotted his treatment with the following note attached. "Hold for three weeks and reject."

— *Rob Phillips*
  Sunriver, Oregon

I knew at age five that I would be a writer; I just didn't know then what kind. It was as a UCLA junior, when I decided to try writing for the *Daily Bruin* newspaper and took to it like a duck to water, that I knew.

Since then, I've written hundreds of articles for the *Los Angeles Times* and various magazines, mostly about entertainment and figure skating, all freelance. At the beginning of my professional career, I sometimes thought that entertainment journalism was a somewhat frivolous way to make a living—until I realized that during my own tough times, I'd always escaped into entertainment reading for emotional rescue. And in good times, it's fun—and educational—to learn more about the diversions you like.

I've subsequently seen first-hand the effect my writing has had, sometimes positive, sometimes dubious. The attention paid Nancy Kerrigan via my November 1993 *Skating* magazine cover story was cited by rival Tonya Harding's camp as one reason for Kerrigan's world-famous knee-clubbing two months later. But articles on social issues have generated thousands of dollars of reader donations for worthy causes.

Clearing out decades-old files recently, I came across a note from an *L.A. Times* writer I'd met, to whom I'd submitted a pitch and my sole professional clip. While his section wasn't then accepting freelance work, "that shouldn't discourage you from a life in journalism," he wrote. "I honestly think you have real potential. I wish you luck. Cheers."

Cheers, indeed.

— *Libby Slate*
  Los Angeles, California

The writing life seems so glamourous to the outside world, when it really is good hard work. But it also is the only way to share wonderful experiences with friends you don't know you have. My husband, Michael Larsen, and I created the series of *Painted Ladies* books—photographic books featuring Victorian homes painted in many colors. We did the first one almost by accident. We fell in love with the Rainbow streets. No one in California would buy the book—it was too expensive. Everyone in NYC thought that the book was regional.

But the book did sell, and little did we know that we had started something that America is still experiencing! People started writing to us from all over the country, sending photographs of their newly painted houses.

Ten years later, we decided to do another book, *Daughters of Painted Ladies*, and traveled around America. It was a wonderful experience, meeting people who were fans, who were beautifying their world. We went from town to town along both coasts and in the midwest, the south, the east. We gave slide shows to historical societies and were hosted in beautiful B & B's. We discovered that America was wonderful.

After three more books and ten years, we put together *America's Painted Ladies* and saw how the face of America had changed, how all kinds of houses and businesses—even skyscrapers—now incorporated color into their facades. That extra stripe of color here or shading there—what we call "the Painted Ladies effect."

But what we most remember is the friends we've made and the positive changes we've made on the face of America. Writing really can change the world!

— *Elizabeth Pomada*
San Francisco, California

The Glamorous Book Party as a Cautionary Tale

It was meant to be a glamorous affair, and there was no arguing by the looks of it that it was. The December 2005 book launch for my Frommer's Buenos Aires First Edition was held at the Argentine Consulate in New York City, a belle-epoque building where Arthur Frommer himself introduced me with a magnificent keynote speech. But when I made it to the stage, somehow, the lights got turned off and I gave my talk in the dark. Later, I made my way through crowds downing Malbec as they watched live tango dancers. With about 500 guests, the party was one of New York's largest ever book events. Still, I distinctly recall crazy Park Avenue matrons with too much plastic surgery and mink coats painfully jabbing me in the arm to get my attention to sign their copies of the book, frustrated that I was talking with my own friends. The Consulate's staircase was one of those sweeping constructions you could imagine Evita herself walking down in a Dior dress, but I remember instead a confrontation on the landing with a fellow travel writer complaining to me about the food. I imagine he was voicing his anger at me not because I was the event host, but instead because he thought I was one of the cater-waiters. Yes, being a writer is glamorous, but I always tell this story as a cautionary tale. The writer's life has many sides and frustrations, even if, outwardly, it seems a success.

— *Michael Luongo*
  New York, New York

This happened many years ago, but I've never forgotten it. I had traveled to a small town in the Texas Hill Country on assignment for a home magazine. In the article, there was a mention of some handcrafted rugs at one of the local stores. After the story appeared, I received a long, heartfelt, handwritten letter from a woman who, as it turned out, was the designer and weaver. But this was no ordinary thank you note. She said that she had decided to give up her craft because sales were so slow, and she was tired. The mere mention of her rugs in a national magazine had literally brought her business back to life, the orders were pouring in, and she felt that she was going to be able to make it. We had never met, and I was touched that she had taken the time to write. The letter reinforced what I've always known but sometimes forget: the power of the printed word to affect lives in ways that can't be anticipated. It was a small thing, no newsworthy event, no eloquent or grandiose prose, no great cause or crusade – just a few simple words that altered someone's life. When I get tired, or discouraged, or wonder why I do what I do, I think about that letter, that woman, and those rugs that had their moment in the sun, and I feel better.

— *Julie Catalano*
  San Antonio, Texas

Like many members in ASJA I didn't choose writing as a career path, it chose me. At the age of 9 I sat down and started scribbling a novel called *Marcy and the New Girl*. It turned into *Marcy and the Lost Girl* as the 106-page handwritten (mostly in pencil!) novel was accidentally thrown out during a move; but I was hooked. Being a writer is like being a cat—you are endlessly resurrected. A rejection from one magazine doesn't mean it won't be accepted by another. And one form of journalism can morph into another. For instance, cushy travel writing assignments such as 'roughing' it at the Copacabana in Rio de Janeiro led to my ripping my eyes off the spectacular sunsets and noticing the street children no one seemed to care about. I wound up writing not about paradise but about the *favelas* (ghettos). This article, published in *Hemispheres*, led to cash and volunteers flooding in to help these children. I have since published articles about street kids in Romania, 'witches' camps in Ghana, how mosquito nets in poor African villages can save millions of lives, etc. Sure I still do pieces that quickly wind up as bird cage liners (I enjoy being paid to lap up a Margarita in Mexico as much as the next person) but knowing that my words can occasionally make a difference in people's lives has made a profound difference in mine.

— *Sherry Amatenstein*
New York, New York

In 1989 or 1990 I spoke on a members' day panel, "Writing West of the Hudson." After explaining that projects in Washington DC sometimes used language such as "150 condoms per man-year" (for a fertility project), I said, "The more boring the project, the more you charge." Later Dorothy Beach, who ran our Dial-a-Writer service, called to ask if I was interested in helping an elderly man in Ohio write his life story. (Dorothy had written "funny, boring" next to my name, and assumed Ohio meant "boring." Or did she mean I was?) I flew to Dayton, rented a car, drove to New Bremen, and learned that at a lunch with Kitty Kelley (won through a silent auction for charity), the family had been advised by Kitty to use ASJA to find a writer. (Thank you, Kitty, Dorothy, and ASJA!) Of those interviewed for the job, the family decided to "go with the middle-aged woman." My client, Jim Dicke II, was an absolute dream. When I proposed making the life story of his grandfather, Warren Webster, the vehicle for a social history about the transportation lift industry, Jim said, "Go for it." Later I wrote the story of Jim's lift truck firm and a history of the Young Presidents' Organization. Kitty's lunch and my talk led me to a whole new career: helping people write their life stories and writing histories of organizations. Moral: Accept speaking engagements, be willing to shift writing gears.

— *Pat McNees*
Bethesda, Maryland

I Was a Chinese Ghost

The January 2, 2000 issue of *The New York Times Magazine* carried an article by Gish Gen in its food section on Grace Zia Chu, author of *The Pleasures of Chinese Cooking* and *Madame Chu's Chinese Cooking School*, who died in 1999. Gen explained that one could trace the Americanization of Madame Chu through the way she referred to her people—"we Chinese" in the first book and "the Chinese" in the second.

There was only one problem with this theory: Dan Chu, Grace's son, ghosted the first book and I, a fourth-generation American, the second. It hardly occurred to me to say "we Chinese." Years later, I met Gish Gen and explained the change in terminology.

I had taken Mrs. Chu's basic Chinese cooking course a few years before I ran into her at a New York Wellesley Club function (she was Class of '24 or '25; I was a little later than that). "You writer?" she asked. I said, yes, I was writer. It seemed Simon and Schuster, the publishers of her first book, wanted another book and Dan was not available. I was offered the job.

I didn't get rich or famous, but I've never had more fun. In Pennsylvania Dutch country, I assisted Mrs. Chu as she taught the locals how to make spring rolls. I tried out recipes on my Viennese husband, and my father loved introducing his friends to "my daughter, the Chinese ghost."

— *Bettijane Eisenpreis*
New York, New York

Nothing to Do With Travel?

I had written obituaries, features and sports, but I never thought of writing travel until a friend announced UCLA was offering a 6-week course in travel writing and why didn't we attend. With years of traveling around the globe under my belt, I was enticed.

My first article has remained one of my biggest hits. It featured the "Waiver" theaters in LA as an evening alternative for those coming to the city for the 1984 Olympics,. In a phenomenon unique to Los Angeles, New York and San Francisco, over 100 tiny houses, seating 99 or less, waive Equity union wages to showcase top film and stage talent at bargain prices.

The article ran in some of the top newspapers in the country, including the *Chicago Tribune* and *Philadelphia Inquirer*. Since I was successful at the top, I decided to try some second tier publications, starting with the *Kansas City Star*. The travel editor sent me a rejection, stating, "This has nothing to do with travel." My internal response: "What do you know!" became my mantra for all future rejections.

My favorite anecdote came from *The San Francisco Examiner*. Upon receiving my submission packet the editor called and asked if I had any interesting photos of theaters. I didn't, since most were bare store fronts, but three months later, walking along Melrose Avenue, I found one that seemed unique. I called the *Examiner* to ask if they'd still like a photo? "Oh," the editor replied, "didn't you know, we ran the article three months ago." But I hadn't received payment—a fact I quickly rectified!

But that wasn't the end of the story. One year later, in my original SASE, I received a rejection letter from *The San Francisco Examiner*, stating, "Sorry, we could not use your article."

— *Judy Florman*
   Santa Ana, California

The assignment was from *Cat Fancy*. I had queried the editor on a Phoenix-area animal rescue service—I would do a profile of him and his cat rescues. He was a fireman moonlighting for extra cash for his growing family (his wife was pregnant at the time, so I came with gift in hand). I would shadow him on a few rescues, take photos and write up a 1,200-word article. No problem.

The subject was most accommodating—gave me a lengthy interview, introduced me to his family and arranged various photo ops. Everything was hunky dory, as they say, until I handed in the piece. The editor was taking her time getting it to press, and I was looking forward to a decent byline and, of course, the money.

But fate intervened as I was reading the local newspaper over breakfast one morning at the neighborhood big box store. On the front page, no less, was an article detailing the perversions of my "squeaky-clean," hard-working fireman. He was accused of molesting children. That's the moment I put down my coffee and naively asked my husband, "You think he did it?" He laughed. He knew what I was about to find out—it didn't matter if he did it or not. I was screwed, and the story was toast.

So I informed the editor that my fireman had morphed into a sex pervert and pulled the story. No money and no kudos. And the piece de resistance? A few months later, the subject called and innocently asked me when the story would run. Duh....

— *Janice Arenofsky*
  Scottsdale, Arizona

I was doing a freelance piece about the enduring popularity of the *Three Stooges* and happened to mention it to Bob Anderson (after whom the ASJA's Robert C. Anderson Memorial Award is named). Bob told me he once interviewed Moe Howard, Larry Fine, and whoever the third Stooge was at the time over lunch at one of Chicago's fancier restaurants.

By then their 1930s and '40s movie shorts had been revived on TV and they'd become icons to many of us baby boomers. Bob, however, knew next to nothing about their act, so he asked around and learned that it largely involved Moe, the lead Stooge, abusing the other two.

"What's this thing you do where you poke somebody in the eyes?" Bob innocently asked Moe, hoping, I suppose, for a good quote.

"Oh, you mean this?" said Moe, jabbing his index and middle fingers into Larry's eye sockets, much to the horror of half the restaurant.

For a Stooge fan like me, it was one of those episodes in another writer's life that I would have happily traded for. If only Bob's next question had been: "And what's this I hear about pie fights?"

— *Greg Daugherty*
Mamaroneck, New York

Writing: What is it Good For?

On a Camden Town afternoon, drifting on autopilot, I asked a shop proprietor for her business card. "Why?" she challenged. "Uh, I'm from Canada, a travel writer." The forty-something redhead erupted: "The last thing we want is more Canadians here! The Canadian dollar isn't worth anything!" Oops.

Pursued by shrieking, I wove to the curb among the pretty reproduction tables, tasseled throws, and porcelain eggs—so welcoming minutes before. "I've already told the Embassy!" The Embassy? I began taking notes. "Write that down! You can write, can't you?" Yes, I can.

Still, I was upset. Was this anti-colonialism? Oh god, was it me? Next door, among antique prints and maps, a smiling owner awaited. "What are you writing?" My story got ladles of sympathy, a trait that counters the English Scold: Aiding in a Crisis. He rolled his eyes, he sighed; he offered a free Sunday walking tour. "She's offended more people than I've had hot dinners," said a third storeowner, knocking several pounds off some Deco cutlery. "I've had people come to me from her in tears."

Thereafter I became mildly obsessed with documenting the Scold: "Please Queue on the Right," "Don't Touch," "Mind the Gap," and my favorite, at Heathrow, a lengthy discourse that culminated: "Don't Abuse the Security Staff." Security duly approached. "Why, Madam, are you photographing our sign?" I explained I was a collector of English signs. She let me go, with a scolding.

— *Nancy Wigston*
  Georgetown, Ontario, Canada

The house was near the entrance to a suburban tract and way too neat. When I asked the man who'd invited me over about this, he pulled a face and admitted that it was a model home he was renting.

"I'm getting a divorce," he said. "It's just temporary."

He'd called me to introduce himself as a wealthy coin dealer who had a great story for me. I was West Coast Editor of *Soldier of Fortune Magazine*—in other words, the managing editor took my calls—and so I listened as he talked about his Vietnam days as a Green Beret. Finally I asked him to get to the point: What was the great story?

"I want to be a mercenary," he said. "Just for a year or two. I need you to give me a connection, somebody who hires mercenaries."

I didn't know anybody like that. I covered US unconventional forces. Anyway, it was a felony to recruit mercenaries for foreign governments.

He pulled out a briefcase and counted out $10,000 in hundreds.

"Sorry, but I can't help you," I said.

He counted out $10,000 more and laid it all in front of me.

"All I need is a phone number."

I mumbled something about other plans and fled.

The next morning I caught two FBI agents behind my house, going through my garbage. They ran.

When I told my editor about it, he laughed. "Betcha it was an FBI sting. Got your file through Freedom of Information."

It took three years to get the file, but he was right. The FBI ran a sting, and I didn't bite.

End of story.

— *Marvin Wolf*
Los Angeles, California

I believe that no writer since the authors penned the *Holy Bible* has had the experience I had with my novel, *Second Chances*.

My editor, who really liked this book, did not like the name of my heroine, Harriet. He claimed that it was "too old" for my protagonist, the early-fifties mother of grown daughters.

I always listen to police offers, internists and editors. I assume they know their business and I'll learn something. This is what I learned from my editor: *Never change the name of a character.*

When the copy-edited manuscript came back to me, I crossed out every Harriet the copy-editor had missed, and replaced it with Julie, the name we'd agreed on. (This was before Search and Replace, which would have prevented the ultimate catastrophe.)

I crossed out all the Harriets, but warned my editor that an author's eyes are not always twenty-twenty when it comes to her own words. Not to worry! Another read-through in the production department would catch what I'd missed.

As you may already suspect, the book was published with Julie becoming Harriet on one page and Harriet becoming Julie on another. Throughout.

That's not the end of it, unfortunately. This novel is still in print, and too often, I get emails from readers. They range from fury to amusement, to questions about my heroine's latent schizophrenia—or mine. These should go into a volume of their own; they make you laugh, make you cry, and make such good reading.

— *Marlene Fanta Shyer*
  Larchmont, New York

My Greatest Failure as a Journalist... My Greatest Success As A Journalist... Same Story

"The Amazing Legacy Of Michael Patrick Smith" was the most important story I ever wrote. Yet, at one point, it turned out to be the major failure of my career.

I wanted to write an article that would reveal the abuse and neglect that goes on in all too many nursing homes. For years my mother was a resident of different nursing homes. It was a nightmare.

I sent several ideas to the editor I worked with at the *Reader's Digest*. But he rejected each one. Finally he assigned the story.

A young man named Michael Patrick Smith was living in the youth wing of a nursing home where the youngsters were neglected and abused. He sued the owners of the institution. Other young residents joined what became a class action suit. After a twelve-year court battle the suit was lost. In a triumphant turnabout, it was won on appeal.

The *Digest* paid me in full but never published my article. I was devastated. Then, in the greatest victory of my career, I sold the story as the basis for the award-winning ABC television movie "When You Remember Me".

Movie critic John Leonard of *New York* magazine wrote, "'When You Remember Me'...is less a movie about a specific disease than a cry of rage about the shame of our nursing homes—our punishing of the sick as if they were sinful."

— *Rena Dictor LeBlanc*
Sherman Oaks, California

ARTnews magazine sent me to interview Oscar Niemeyer in 1995. Brazil's modernist colossus scheduled the meeting for mid-morning in his Rio de Janeiro office, an unmarked beachfront Copacabana residential building. The buzzer wasn't working. When a neighbor shuffled out, I slipped inside.

Latin America's most famous architect invited me into his office: a cluttered desk wedged behind a divider. He refused to talk, claiming he hadn't been forewarned.

I called his bluff. He'd pulled that one on a colleague.

He shifted gears: a book about him had come out full of mistakes. The author "sent me the manuscript as I'd asked. But I didn't have time to go over it," he said. So no interview.

I pressed on. "I don't want to talk about architecture. Let's talk about soccer," he said. Sportstalk is usually a good male bonding tactic, so I was hopeful. I asked about his favorite team: "I don't root for any particular team anymore. I root for anybody who scores goals."

We moved to baseball. He'd taken in a game in New York (Ebbetts Field? Yankee Stadium? the Polo Grounds?) before the State Department banned his entry into the US as a card carrying Communist. It was "total confusion." But Cubans love baseball, I said, hoping, maybe, to slide the conversation to politics.

He asked me about Clinton's Cuba policy before we moved on to boxing: Mike Tyson was a victim of the system for his rape conviction.

Okay. Never mind.

— *Bill Hinchberger*
  Sao Paulo, Brazil

[Adapted from Bill Hinchberger's online travel guide BrazilMax.com]

When *The 10 Smartest Decisions a Woman Can Make Before 40* was published in Spanish, the Spanish publisher, Pearson Educacion, sponsored book tours for me in Mexico (five cities plus the International Book Fair for a week in Guadalajara), Columbia (3 cities) and Costa Rica. It was wonderful beyond my wildest dreams. Imagine: press conferences in each city, with 30-40 members of the press, TV and radio. Five to eight radio and TV shows per day. Speaking to an audience of 1,000 women at the "Workshop 2000" in Mexico City on, and another 500 young women at the University in Monterrey. I was mobbed at several book signings, with long, long lines. Truly a writer's dream, even through a translator!!!

The funniest moment was when I was to appear on TV Azteca, in Mexico City—the biggest national channel. The show was like our *Today* show (called *Consello De Mujer—The Stamp of a Woman*, which means women's style). While we were waiting to go on, we were watching the taping, and they had a poor unhappy kangaroo, in a harness, who had chafed herself against the leash trying to get loose. It was a sad sight. The kangaroo was pooping all over the floor, and during the segment, the gorgeous TV personality tried to feed the kangaroo biscuits (Purina kangaroo chow?). But it was not cooperating. So, when I got onto the set, and was being miked, and the same woman said to me that she was excited about my book, and thought we would have a great segment, I said, "I'll probably be easier than the kangaroo." I thought she was going to fall off the couch, she laughed so hard, and she almost didn't get herself back together before the camera came on. A very fun moment.

— *Tina B. Tessina, Ph.D.*
Long Beach, California

Weird Stories from the Writing Life

When I was doing a book tour for *The Marriage Map*, my agent darkly hinted she was "sitting on a bomb" and couldn't wait to tell me about it when I got home. But another writer called me first, warning that the agent was up to no good: she was trying to force a young woman to write a book betraying the President of the United States! Fair enough, I suppose, but my agent was being accused of engineering matters in a most unethical way, while becoming embroiled in payment issues as well. It sounded far-fetched, but since the words "ethics" and "pay" always get my attention, I decided to check it out. I asked my agent about the story, and she attacked me for being liberal in my politics. I couldn't figure out what this had to do with our relationship . . . until I learned that the young woman in question was, indeed, the president's lover, and my agent had a sideline as a none-too-reputable conservative operative who was more interested in unseating a democrat than in agenting books. So we parted ways. My book was a bestseller. The agent never got a tell-all out of the young woman, who made a big splash but eventually faded into history.

— *Maxine Rock*
  Atlanta, Georgia

My old freelance marketing method must seem painfully naive now, but it's how I started: I'd write an essay, decide who might like to print it, and send it in the mail with a brief note and a SASE. Then I'd wait. I learned over time that a phone call was good (the editor had some interest) and the mailbox was bad (the despised rejection slip). Computers were novelties. So I was excited one afternoon when a phone call came from *The New York Times*. "I have your op-ed piece, and I don't know whether to print it or throw it away," said the editor. I felt like saying, "Let me think it over and get back to you." It was a piece about growing up as a Jewish Arab, proud of the religion and the heritage but not truly accepted by either Jew or Arab. I'd worked hard on it, filled it with history, humor, pathos and a call for tolerance. "I'll tell you what," he said, "it's 1,200 words. If you can give me 600 words by tomorrow I'll run it." Almost tearfully I surgically trimmed my baby (as I saw all my stories) and delivered a 604-word infant. It drew attention in New York and around the world. A woman with an accent called: "With this story you will be welcomed anywhere in the Arab world," she said. This year, 25 years later, I'm planning my first trip to accept that invitation.

— *Herbert Hadad*
  Pleasantville, New York

Finding an agent who's a perfect fit for a book proposal is crucial for any writer. I learned this the hard way in 1993 when I began working with a highly recommended agent in New York City. She agreed to try to sell my book proposal on the Great Smoky Mountains National Park, near my home in Knoxville.

She wasn't having much success, and when I asked her where she had submitted the proposal, she was very vague. She offered only that an editor at Simon & Schuster had indeed been interested at one point, but the editor doubted one of my facts. "And frankly," the agent said in a point-blank tone, "I'm a bit skeptical, too. You say that the Smokies is the most visited national park in the country. Where did you get that?"

"From the park service," I answered. "It's a very common statistic. Nine million people a year visit this park."

"Come on, Katy," she answered in a very irritated tone. "You mean to tell me that the Smokies gets more visitors than Disney World?"

It took a moment for me to regain my composure, but then I replied, "We're talking national parks here, not amusement parks."

"I knew that," the agent shot back instantly in a very crisp, professional tone before launching into a completely different topic.

I immediately realized that although this agent might have done a great job for many other writers, she was giving me and my proposal strictly Mickey Mouse service.

— *Katy Koontz*
Knoxville, Tennessee

Years ago, my husband and I went to NY to see Peter Falk playing in *The Prisoner of Second Avenue*. I wrote, giving the date we'd be at the show and asked for an interview. He never answered.

Backstage after the show, I told the stage manager that I had an interview with Peter Falk. He told us to wait, then came back and said to follow him. We did, ending up in Falk's dressing room.

He grinned that familiar crooked smile and said, "I didn't think you'd really show up...but since you're here, sit down."

I was in awe and speechless. My husband came to my rescue, saying, "I understand you went to the University of Wisconsin. Me too."

"Oh," said Falk, "it was a great school...." and the two of them traded memories. I "came to" and tried to be professional, asking questions and taking notes in my brand new reporter's notebook.

Six months later, the phone rang just as I was piling our five kids into the car to leave for the beach. I answered the phone abruptly on the third ring.

"This is *Screen Star* magazine . . ." the voice on the other end began.

"I have all the magazines I want," about to hang up.

"But . . . we want to buy your Falk article," the voice said.

And they did. It was the strangest experience I've ever had—both with the interview and almost hanging up on the editor—even now after writing 21 books and hundreds of articles.

— *Elaine Fantle Shimberg*
  Tampa, Florida

When I finally nabbed a cover story assignment for my dream market, *Reader's Digest*, I was walking on air. I live in Chappaqua, New York, home of the *Digest's* global headquarters and genuflect as I pass the campus each morning while carpooling my son to school. Yes, RD has a Pleasantville mailing address but according to legend, it's only because the Chappaqua post office was too small to hold its mail. So I was in seventh heaven when "my issue" was prominently displayed at each checkout aisle at the supermarket in our tiny hamlet. I was thrilled that copies were simultaneously being dropped into mailboxes all around my neighborhood. Yet my journalistic coup went unnoticed. No one I knew acknowledged seeing my story.

That same month we had a family crisis. My husband's *routine* cardiac stress test turned out to be anything but. Only hours afterward, he underwent emergency angioplasty. Luckily, he recuperated quickly and wrote a brief, but gracious letter to the editor of the local throwaway newspaper complimenting the medical care he received at our hospital, which was struggling to survive.

A couple of days later, we both walked into a liquor store next to the supermarket to purchase a celebratory bottle of champagne. As my husband signed the check, the clerk asked him if he was the same Jerome Levine whose letter had appeared in the newspaper. I felt totally deflated until I found out that the clerk moonlighted as an EMT for the hospital.

— *Irene S. Levine, Ph.D.*
Chappaqua, New York

I never write celebrity profiles. Ever. Here's why. Years ago Mid Atlantic magazine asked me to write a profile of Sissy Spacek. "Sure," I said. "Why not? She lives here in my hometown. I see her everywhere—peering into microwave ovens at Sears, shopping at local boutiques. She'd be easy to catch, I thought.

"You'll never get the interview," warned my friend, another local writer who tried and failed to get an interview with the Oscar winner.

What a challenge, I thought. I'd get that interview.

I phoned her mother-in-law, who was her manager, as well as director Jack Fisk's mom. "Oh, Sissy would love to be interviewed," she said, in her charming, southern drawl. "But call again." I called again and again and again and got the same, saccharin-sweet answer.

Then, one day, I went to pick my husband up at our small airport. Low and behold, there was a tiny, three-year-old replica of Sissy Spacek in the waiting room with her grandma (probably the mother-in-law I'd been pestering).

The first person off the plane was Sissy—followed by my husband, who was grinning ear-to-ear. "Guess who I sat next to on the plane," he gushed. Of course it was Sissy and they chatted all the way. "I told her you wanted to interview her," he said. "I'd loved to be interviewed—sometime," she replied. But sometime never arrived.

— *Judy Mandell*
   North Garden, Virginia

Can't Stop Us from Writing

"**L**isten to this", I said to my mother as she was cooking. I read her my poem that had been accepted by *Jack and Jill.* "That's terrible," she commented, not knowing I was the author. At 10 years old, I was devastated.

I have had other traumatic writing situations. When I first started out as a medical writer at *The Star-Ledger* in Newark, NJ, I received a call from a volunteer at the Veterans Hospital. She told me about a "veteran who cries on holidays" because his wife and children were living in a rural New Jersey shack without adequate food or facilities. Indeed, I found his family was living in dire circumstances so I wrote a story about: "The Veteran Who Cries on Holidays."

It became a national story and the phone lines at *The Ledger* were so clogged that correspondents had trouble filing their stories. The next day in the newsroom I received a call from a detective who asked me: "Do you really know why this guy is in the hospital?"

My mistake was not to find out! I had assumed it was because of depression but learned he was there as a plea deal because he had molested an 11 year old girl. The money and the calls were pouring in and the veteran decided to sign himself out of the hospital to take advantage of the situation. Fortunately, it was before Watergate-wannabe-journalists and my city editor was still straight out of Front Page.

"Don't worry!" he said, and arranged to buy the Veteran Who Cries at Holidays a car. He gave the family the rest of the money collected and shipped them all back to the Southern state from which they had emigrated.

Thirty-seven books, hundreds of articles and two syndicated columns later, I am still writing.

— *Ruth Winter*
Short Hills, New York

On my first individual press trip as a travel writer, I thought my husband and nephew did a pretty good job of wrecking my budding career. We got to Bald Head Island—and our fabulous private rental home—at dusk. Cars were not allowed on the island, so my husband ran into the garage like a little boy eager to try driving the golf cart. With no light on in the garage, he pressed the accelerator and crashed into the back wall of the garage, dislodging the large electric battery charger on a shelf over the cart. The charger fell through the windshield. Once I ascertained my husband was fine, I was a wreck. How could I explain this lack of professional behavior to my PR host, outside of paying for all the damage, of course. Meanwhile, my 12-year-old nephew took it upon himself to change all the clocks in the house to coincide with the fall time change, dropping the special clock that also recorded the tide timetable. I was beside myself.

After all damages were paid for, and all was said and done, I realized getting freebies for writing a travel story was not all that great—at least not if my family was involved. It was a long time before they were invited on a trip again. But after my friend Gretchen set fire to the sheet at the Beverly Hills Hotel on a girlfriends' getaway trip I was reporting, I figured accidents can happen to anyone, and at least they are fodder for making my experience unique.

— *Judy Kirkwood*
  Fitchburg, Wisconsin

Some of my major writing projects have had their roots in a minor article in a weekly newspaper or in a conversation only vaguely connected to the subject about which I later wrote. For example, on a spring day in 1995 I read a three-paragraph article announcing a dinner scheduled to celebrate the opening of the Seabrook Educational and Cultural Center in Upper Deerfield, New Jersey and to recognize the fiftieth anniversary of the arrival of 2,500 Japanese Americans from internment camps to work at Seabrook Farms. I clipped the article, and a few weeks later visited the newly opened museum.

After considerable research that included many interviews with men and women representing 25 nations or cultures who had worked at Seabrook Farms (*LIFE* magazine called it the "biggest vegetable factory on earth"), I wrote the book *Growing a Global Village: Making History at Seabrook Farms* (Holmes & Meier, 2003).

— *Charles "Chick" Harrison*
Woodstown, New Jersey

Any writer who has balanced working from home while parenting young children can relate to my story. I've been freelancing as a journalist and book author for 18 years, and my babies are now 14 and 18. But in the early-1990s it was still professionally unacceptable to be a work-at-home mom. So I went to great lengths to pretend that I worked in a "real" office and the noises in the background were the office janitors. For the most part, I was successful. Houdini has nothing on me. For instance, on one particularly crazy balancing-it-all day, I interviewed a well known author while simultaneously wiping my four-year-old's bottom and nursing my infant. The article came out great, I'm proud to say, and the author never had a clue. (Don't ask about the sanitary conditions, please. We working moms do what we have to.) Then there was the time a politician finally returned my call as I played with my 18-month-old. She, who had stopped nursing months before and had never used the following words, announced, "Mommy, I want to eat your nipples." I pretended she hadn't spoken and continued the interview, praying he hadn't heard. But my daughter felt it necessary to say it again, louder—and directly into the phone. She won; I ended the call. Mothering and humility are incompatible.

Now that my daughters are older, naturally, it's more acceptable that we writers work at home. Those years of juggling both weren't easy, but they were worth every embarrassing minute.

— *Liza N. Burby*
  Huntington Station, New York

The best freelance writing job I ever had in terms of creative expression was writing video scripts in the late 1970s that taught public school teachers how to do educational research using ERIC, an educational computer database—a novelty in 1979. Our local board of education hired me as a freelance writer to work with producers and narrators to create these documentary videos.

The time period kicked off the computer age for educational researchers. A popular TV and radio personality narrated my scripts—a fact that made me proud—and freelance producers pulled the ropes and put the show on the road. As a freelance writer, my pay was $500 per script.

Those were the days I would have written scripts for that kind of money just for the experience of working with a team producing educational documentaries that made a difference. After the script writing came an assignment to write a 500-page business guide for the county education center. I also wrote a grant to build a school/center for life long continuing adult education and other freelance writing assignments.

My next favorite freelance job was writing press releases about a software program, for which I was paid $500 a page. The market is changing today with different needs and payscales for freelancing in California. But those were my favorite writing days. Today I'm a print-on-demand published historical novelist and author of 85 how-to books.

— *Anne Hart*
   Sacramento, California

When *The New York Times* published my essay "A Hometown Boy Returns" in April 1985, I believed that my dreams of success as a writer were within my grasp. This tale of a native son torn from his New York roots was destined to become a novel. During the next two decades, I would discover the sobering realities about such great expectations. Ultimately, the goals you realize may be far more modest and meaningful than those you set out to achieve. In spring 1985, I was living in Cleveland, working in the communications industry and freelancing on the side. But my true love as a writer lay on the mystical shores of fiction. By the early 1990s, my marriage had ended, my freelance business had plateaued after a five-year run, and I had entered grad school as a 40-year-old. In 1995, I began my novel, *Delamore's Dreams,* about a prodigal son and his estranged father fighting for respect (and each other) in a gritty New York community in the 1960s. During the next decade, I would remarry, become a stepfather and university professor, write dozens more articles and stories, and publish a 2004 book of literary journalism on social activism, *Inspired to Serve: Today's Faith Activists* (Indiana Univ. Press). A year later, my novel was published, completing the literary quest I had dreamed of 20 years earlier when *The New York Times* raised the hopes of an aspiring author.

— *Mark H. Massé*
Muncie, Indiana

King Lear? Who He?

Shari Steiner, a fellow ASJA member, interviewed me and other tax mavens for an article on investment strategies that ran in a 2000 issue of *New Choices,* a now defunct magazine. Shari included my comments about complicated tax issues that are often overlooked when parents make substantial gifts of personal residences and other assets to their children. In particular, she cited my admonition to clients "not to adopt this strategy without first seeing a performance of *King Lear.*"

My seemingly unsubtle warning prompted a call from the article's fact checker—someone so clueless that she asked what a King Lear was. The newest selection at Burger King was the first response that came to mind. But mindful of how Shari and many other members had often helped me, I decided to be more forthcoming.

Identifying the play's author and summarizing the plot surely would be an easy way to resolve things. Major mistake; identification and summarization were followed by a lengthy silence. Fortunately, *Shakespeare In Love* had recently been released. A mention of Gwyenth Paltrow was sufficient to satisfy the checker.

— *Julian Block*
  Larchmont, New York

I made myself an expert on whales and ended up selling 10 books and more than 250 articles on them. The first few books were sold by a top agent, but the best book deal I've had was when I turned to ants. My agent rejected it so I negotiated it myself and found myself in the middle of an auction with four top New York houses. The result was a six figure deal including a film sale, translations into Japanese and Chinese, book clubs, and other subsidiary sales. Who would have thought that ants would sell better than whales?

— *Erich Hoyt*
  North Berwick, Scotland

Writing suits me perfectly. I love the nonexistent dress code, the solitude, and the endless opportunity to ponder. Being self-employed, I couldn't ask for a nicer, more understanding boss. Above all, the job is never dull.

My most startling assignment came twenty-five years ago. A school board official called to ask if I might be interested in some work. He could not describe the assignment except to caution that it was top secret. To learn more, I'd need to come to a meeting at headquarters downtown.

At the time, I was in manic start-up mode, trying to learn about the business while writing articles for newspapers and magazines and working on my first novel. Through it all, I clung fast to my guiding literary principle: anything for a buck.

The building was a stodgy Federal brick. I was ushered to a garishly lit conference room. The superintendent, an imposing figure, sat at the head of the scarred table. It was just the two of us, and for a minute, I had the dislocating sense that I must have done something really bad.

Leaning in, he folded his thick hands. "Here's the thing, Ms. Kelman. This job requires a great deal of writing: speeches, reports, not to mention my weekly column for the local paper."

"So you're looking for help?"

"You bet I am. I can't write worth a damn."

For two years, I ghosted his column, reports, and speeches. Then naturally, he moved on to bigger, more powerful educational job.

— *Judith Kelman*
New York, New York

Run, Rabbit, Run

I never wanted to be a racecar driver, although many motorsports writers itch to get behind the wheel at a track. All that changed for me when covering a Grand Prix at Watkins Glen, where Volkswagen staged The Bunny Hop VW Rabbit Media pre-race, providing us with Rabbits and 32 ounces of gas in a glass vial attached to the passenger window. The winner who squeezed the most mileage from this meager ration won a trip to the Bahamas.

We queued up neatly at the starting line. Nearby was Ahmad Sadiq, art director for *Penthouse* magazine, with a stable of voluptuous models draped over the hood of his fire-engine red Rabbit. Admiring them was Rabbit-less Junius Chambers, *New York Amsterdam News*. His entry had been stolen in Manhattan the night before.

The starter gun popped. Halfway around, my car coughed, choked, and sputtered to an ignominious stop.

"Hey, lady," shouted a rude spectators, "step on the gas!"

A track mechanic ran over. "Get a move on, lady! You can't stop there! Oh," he said. "You've got an air bubble. I'll blow it out." He inserted the plastic tube between his lips and inhaled. The air bubble disappeared, along with half my bottle of gas.

"Hey! You've swallowed my ration!" I yelled. Fifty feet from the finish line, with one final gurgle, my gasless Rabbit stopped dead. I was towed back to the pits.

The official result rated me with 36 mpg. Bill Turney, *Hartford Courant*, won with 72.8 mpg.

I don't know if the guy who selfishly swallowed my gas perished or, (sorry, God) merely suffered extremely painful spasms. Curiously, I was not invited to race again. I never wanted to be a race driver anyway. Writing about the races was excitement enough. So there.

— *Jill Amadio*
  Dana Point, California

The Writing Life: You Never Know Who You're Going to Reach!

In 1986, I wrote two articles for *Good Housekeeping*'s "New York Metro" column, now defunct. One of my pieces, like all "New York Metro" columns, dealt with a topic only germaine to Manhattan: "Where to find the Women's Room," a rating of 16 public restrooms, mostly in New York's finer hotels. (The Waldorf-Astoria still has the best, in my opinion.)

Fast forward to 1996, I'm having lunch with an editor for whom I worked at *The Patent Trader* newspaper. With us is the editor's mother from Ohio. While dining, the mother remarked that my name seemed familiar to her. She opened up her pocketbook, and lo and behold, in her wallet was a dog-eared article entitled "Where to find the Women's Room!" "Your article saved me and my bladder," commented this spry out-of-towner.

Another article I wrote in 1986 for "New York Metro" involved where to find quiet indoor phone booths. In pre-cell phone days, office building lobbies and hotels used to have booths with seats, writing surfaces, and folding doors for privacy. My article reached a business man from Albany, Georgia who traveled to Manhattan and used my advice on where to find the best phone booths. So grateful, he wrote a fan letter to *Good Housekeeping*, the first male acknowledgment the magazine had received since its inception as a woman's magazine!

— *Wesley C. Davidson*
  Vero Beach, Florida

For one who has written thousands of newspaper articles, hundreds of magazine pieces and half a dozen books, high tech means a vast shift in methods of communications and research. It does not, however, make life any easier. In ways, the high-tech age has only added to our difficulties.

In the old days, that is in the 1960s when I first went to Asia as a freelance, American editors looked with interest on features with exotic datelines. It was possible to accumulate a number of strings and spin off magazine pieces on the side. Incredibly, while the world has expanded, space has diminished dramatically, and the Internet spews out so much stuff as to cut into editor's interest in original pieces.

So what's a freelance to do? One problem in the new information age is the Internet goes anywhere, and you can't spin off the same ideas, and pieces, with quite such wild abandon. You may turn increasingly to writing for websites, but you're taking a risk if you send the same piece to more than one or two tried and true customers.

Another option: commentaries and op-ed pieces. You need a number of outlets to make them viable economically, and lately I've run into a disturbing phenomenon. Would you believe, editors honestly say, fine, love to have the piece, oh, by the way, we can't pay. ASJA members may appreciate my view that I find non-payment, for whatever reason, not only abhorrent and despicable but unethical and immoral.

Funny thing, the ease of Googling facts and stats doesn't necessarily make life easier than before. Or, to put it another way, ready access to background info hardly counterbalances the loss of space and markets.

— *Donald Kirk*
   Washington, D.C.

Although I'm a *New York Times* hardcover bestselling author, and professional writer for 36 years in many forms, one of my most joyous stories is writing about a real author's writing, as a book critic and veteran member of the National Book Critics Circle.

In July, 1991, *The Cleveland Plain Dealer* offered me $75 and the opportunity to review Norman Mailer's new novel, *Harlots Ghost*, of over 1,300 pages. To write about Mr. Mailer's epic fiction!

I spent more than two months reading and rereading the novel, and writing, revising, and finishing the final review of 750 words. As I never had before, I opened with my critical conclusion:

"*Harlot's Ghost* is the finest novel ever written about the CIA."

Most other critics were less appreciative. When *Publishers Weekly* asked Mr. Mailer about the very mixed reviews, he replied: "*Harlot's Ghost* may be a lopsided mountain, but, by God, it is a mountain."

Later, I listened to Mr. Mailer do a reading from the novel. Afterward, I introduced myself, and showed him a copy of my review:

"Oh, yes! I remember it well. Thank you!" And he shook my hand with vigorous appreciation.

In 1992, Random House quoted my definitive, first sentence, on the first page of the Vintage edition.

Writing is darned hard for everyone, and when even the literary genius of Norman Mailer, with a 40-year body of work, is far from properly appreciated, I am exceedingly happy to have provided my very modest support.

— *Paul D. McCarthy*
New York, New York

In Bandit Country

The Cote d'Azur. 1980s. Mid-August. Hot as Hades. Land in Nice. Rent a Peugeot. Drive toward Toulon. No hotel rooms available. Dusk. I panic. Travel agent's door sign says "Fermé." I bang on it. Travel agent is French man and I'm wearing a skimpy travel outfit. Door opens. He hears my plight. "The overnight ferry for Sardinia is leaving at this moment." He'll call ahead and hold it until I get there. I aim the Peugeot toward it and floor it. Heads peer over the railing to see who in Heaven's name they are holding the ship for.

I sleep peacefully on the overnight ferry. But once in Alghergo I discover the Peugeot and I still have a long way to go. It's even hotter here in Sardinia. Scirocco blowing. Peugeot's red warning light glowing. Mountain roads—no railings. Ancient stone walls. Barren hills sparsely settled by dour peasants.

Long drive to Costa Esmeralda, the Aga Khan's fabulous resort.

Porto Cervo!

Civilization!

A concierge!

"A room? You must be kidding! This is high season. The Costa Esmeralda!"

(This is also bandit country. Vendetta country. Prominent citizens have been kidnapped. I don't relish sleeping in the Peugeot.)

I pull out all the stops.

"I'm a journalist with assignments. I need to rest. If you can't get me a room get me the police."

(But one doesn't call for the carabineri here.)

Eureka!

Found: a small room in nearby Olbia.

Moral: When in doubt ask the carabineri.

— *Kay Cassill*
   Providence, Rhode Island

You Never Know

As a food and wine writer I have written articles that ranged from aïoli to Zinfandel. Food trends are always in demand and, over the past 20 years, I have heralded Balsamic vinegar, extra Virgin olive oil, tapas, sushi, and veal cheeks. When the chocolate craze took the public by storm, I proposed an in-depth chocolate article to a cruise line magazine.

"If I get the assignment, I'll be in trouble," I told my husband.

He understood my plight. I had an aversion to chocolate; as a child, the very smell had made me nauseous.

I did get the assignment and started the research. I learned about the types of cocoa beans, plantation terroir, production process, single origin and blended chocolates, styles of individual chocolate makers and, most important, that the best chocolates contain between 60% and 85% pure cocoa beans.

When I was ready for the tasting, I invited two neighbors, figuring that between them and my chocolate loving husband, I could wing the tasting report. Like wine, chocolate is judged by appearance, aroma, texture, mouth feel, flavor and aftertaste. We tasted chocolates from ten different producers. The first sample was a 72% single origin chocolate from Venezuela. It sparkled and snapped; the aroma reminded of raspberries. I let it melt in my mouth and swallowed it slowly. I felt an intense pleasure. It startled me. I tasted the next piece and the following. My appreciation increased with every morsel.

Chocolate. Who knew.

— *Helen Studley*
New York, New York

Not a Prisoner

A few years ago I owned a news service at the Colorado State Capitol. Most of my time was spent translating legalese for the general public.

After hearing about problems in the Women's Prison, a surge of investigative reporter came over me. I decided to get myself committed into the prison to see what was really happening. I knew prison officials from interviewing them, and because my husband was a lawyer, I felt I could surreptitiously get in on fake charges, spend a week inside the prison, and at the appropriate time declare my innocence and be "sprung."

It didn't work quite that way. I asked my husband: "If there are any problems, you'll get me out, won't you?" His answer infuriated me. "I'm sorry, Marilyn, but if you want to do this crazy thing—you're on your own."

In the end, I spent a week inside among the prisoners but returned to my motel at night. I discovered the majority of them were not violent. Most had committed check fraud—trying to get money to feed their families. Two, however, were in prison for killing their husbands in a fit of passion.

I had been upset when my husband said he would not rescue me. However, the experience of being "inside the walls" for five days was devastating. I was grateful I had not pretended to be a prisoner.

I got my story—and it was picked up by the Associated Press.

— *Marilyn Holmes*
Denver, Colorado

They say to write about what you know, but what happens when you get an assignment about something you know nothing about? If you're smart (and brave), you accept and learn fast.

That's what happened with one of my first freelance assignments. An editor at *Institutional Investor* asked me to interview a Wall Street CEO, despite the fact that I didn't know a bull from a bear! Apparently the executive's hobby was gate-crashing! He gave me a fascinating interview replete with anecdotes such as how he'd wangled his way into a front row seat at the UN when the Pope spoke there, and crashed a private party at Johnny Carson's. I left the interview clutching my little tape recorder for the jewels it had recorded—or had it?? As soon as I reached the lobby I turned on the recorder. Nothing!! It was Tylenol® Time for sure! If I failed with my first assignment, the magazine would cross me off its list.

I'd jotted down a few words in my abbreviated shorthand, but they'd mean very little by the time I got home. So I raced across the street to a department store, found a telephone booth, and spent an hour and a half hunched over the inadequate shelf as I transcribed and filled in my nearly illegible notes, abetted by my memory (ignoring the irate customers knocking on the booth window). The editor never knew I'd almost sabotaged myself and the interview was published, netting me a series of assignments. It also netted me a lingering distrust of anything mechanical. (Tip: Always back up those tape recorders with old-fashioned tools known as a notebook and pen!)

— *Anne Hosansky*
   New York, New York

Finding my 15 Minutes of Fame

I've recently branched out into travel writing, and have covered Hong Kong, the Caribbean islands, and other exotic destinations. Little did I realize, however, that local fame for me was not to be born in the streets of Asia or the ports of Grand Turk.

On a lark, I called our newspaper editor and asked if he'd like a travel piece on East Tawas—a destination about ninety minutes by car from my home in central Michigan. Something about that sleepy town with its laid back citizens and their "what you see is what you get" attitude always reminds me of my time in New Zealand. I entitled my article, "East Tawas—Michigan's New Zealand?"

The first surprise came with the great placement and huge spread my editor gave my article and photos. But that was only the beginning. Friends and business associates applauded me, and soon, even people I hardly knew were sending me notes or calling nice comments across super-market aisles. Congratulatory messages stacked up on my answering machine, and natives of East Tawas praised my "capturing the true heart and soul" of the area.

The accolades don't die. Just yesterday I met a neighbor who said she was desperate to visit a Michigan area that was like New Zealand. Gulp! What if she goes there and is disillusioned? After all, East Tawas has no sheep, no Cloudy Bay wineries, and is definitely not close to Australia.

No worries. I'll just fly to Auckland and weave captivating tales about East Tawas.

— *Elyse M. Rogers*
Midland, Michigan

When I was just starting out, I lived in a small city and offered my talents as a ghostwriter. I received a call one day from an English-as-a-Second-Language businessman who asked if I could write a short book for him about the industry he was in. I met him at a restaurant and he described the task.

"I geeve you papers and you make a boook."

"Yes," I said. "That's fine."

"Soom of theese papers they make theese oother companies loook bad."

"Okay," I said. "Every business has competitors. You don't like them."

"Theese is bad men. They do bad things. You put this in the boook."

"I can do that," I said.

"Maybe they do not like the boook."

"That happens," I said.

Now he was coming to the power point. His eyes widened. His finger jabbed the air.

"Maybe they not like boook and they come soot you."

This struck me as exceptionally unsettling. "Whoa," I said. "No shooting. No guns."

"No," he said. "Not shoot. Soot. Soot.,

"Oh," I said, catching his meaning, "'suit.' You mean sue me. . . . Well, Mr. X, I still really don't like the sound of this," and suggested he look for someone else. Lord knows I could have used the work, but, hey, sometimes a little voice inside says to turn it down.

— *Brooke C. Stoddard*
  Alexandria, Virginia

My Feline Journalist

In all my years of living with a cat, I've never been able to train one. My cat Serge was the best example. My husband and I adopted him. He was an athletic streetwise tabby, with big green eyes, who loved living in Chicago. A neighbor said that he often rode the garbage trucks in the morning, perching on the hood. But I got to know him when he began following me around wherever I walked on the streets of the Lakeview neighborhood. When he heard the school bus coming down the street, he'd get scared and run back to our home on Greenview.

When I brought him home I had no idea he wanted to be a journalist. On days I was working on a story in my office, he often bit my bare feet to get my attention. I couldn't ignore him. I had to pay attention to him. I got him some food, or played with him. But many times when I was doing a phone interview with sources, he wanted to ask them questions too. Just when I least expected it, he'd jump on the phone and disconnect me. I'd have to call the source back and apologize. Often they'd tell me they'd heard a meow before the phone went dead. Maybe Serge was asking them a question I had forgotten to ask.

— *Kathleen Vyn*
Chicago, Illinois

Writing some books takes a strong constitution—and can even be emotionally damaging. I was writing *Defy the Darkness*, a nonfiction Holocaust story about a man who endured three death camps and a death march. For 18 months, he also carted out office trash and corpses for Josef Mengele, the notorious "Angel of Death." Midway through my first draft, I started having nightmares. Sometimes, when I stepped into a shower, vivid pictures of death camp showers performing their lethal function would flash into my mind. I lost sleep and concentration. I seriously doubted that I could complete my co-author's story.

While I was still mired in this writing bog, I attended a presentation by Iris Chang, who wrote *The Rape of Nanking*, a horrific Asian Holocaust story. Chang was a slender woman with long, lustrous black hair. She said that while writing *Rape*, she'd been so devastated she'd lost 20 pounds and her hair started falling out. Sometimes a price must be paid for writing such intense books, she said, but publishing them was important despite the personal cost. Her words sufficiently steeled me to finish my own manuscript.

A few years later, Chang, who consistently wrote about difficult topics and was researching a famous WW II death march, committed suicide by gunshot. She was 36 and left behind a husband and two-year-old child. I am still enormously grateful for the resolve to complete my own book that she unknowingly bestowed upon me. I am still profoundly saddened that ultimately she could not offer the gift of that same strength to herself.

— *David Kohn*
   Deerfield, Florida

Over the Transom and Through the Woods....

My proposal for a book about how our daily food choices impact the environment kept bouncing back. How could we get the undivided attention of an editor? I bemoaned our plight to an environmentalist friend of mine who saves rainforests. He was interested in our progress because my co-author and I had promised to share our (as yet imaginary) royalties with his organization, the Center for Ecosystem Survival. "Have you tried Ten Speed Press?" he asked. "Yes," I replied, "and they turned us down." "Well, I may have a contact there," he rejoined.

He did. A few months before this conversation, he had given one of his scheduled presentations. He gives these to schoolkids, adults, zookeepers—anyone who will listen about the dangers facing rainforests. As he entered the room, his heart sank—there were only four people in the audience. But he gave his stump speech anyway and spoke informally to his listeners afterwards.

One of them was a top person at Ten Speed Press.

So now, all these weeks later, he called her up and asked if she would read my proposal. She did and got the rejection overruled. And that's how my book got over the transom and accepted for publication. *Eating to Save the Earth: Food Choices for a Healthy Planet* came out in 2002 and has sold out. Now I'm revising it and looking for its next publisher, never forgetting that the slenderest of threads may lead to success.

And that will be another story.

— *Linda Riebel*
  Lafayette, California

The Perils of Not Being Bombeck

I was about four years into my writing career when a friend snagged me an interview with his very famous agent. Agent Bigname never even got up from behind his enormous desk to shake my hand.

"If you think you're going to be another Erma Bombeck, forget it," he snarled.

I blanched. "No, of course not," I said.

"Because there's never going to be another Erma Bombeck, and, besides, I represent her, and you're no Erma Bombeck."

I tried to switch subjects, particularly because I had wanted to switch genres anyway. So I asked him about what he'd thought about my novel, and he gamely started to fish around for it on his desk, again saying,

"YOU'RE NO ERMA BOMBECK."

"So, what did you think? Would you represent me as a novelist?"

He fetched my manuscript out of his top drawer. It looked so nice, so professional, resplendent beneath its fancy black paper clip.

"Needs a lot of work," said Agent B., "but if you rewrite, sure, I'd do it. Hey, can I keep this?" he said as I got up to leave.

"Of course," I said, smiling at the familiar eighty pages.

Bigname grabbed the giant fancy paper clip from the corner of my manuscript and threw my pages into his garbage can. He fondled the paper clip before setting it down carefully on his desk. Apparently office supplies were more important to him than the egos of fledgling novelists.

— *Cathy Crimmins*
Los Angeles, California

"What do you want to know, honey?" Mel Brooks asked me. "Want me to tell you the truth? Want me to give you the real dirt? Want me to tell you what's in my heart?"

I said yes.

"What would I tell you, really?" he snapped. "That this is the worst movie I've ever seen?" He continued colorfully, throwing in some adjectives based on four-letter words.

When I got my first freelance assignment from *The New York Times*, a piece on the set where Mel Brooks was directing his first feature film, "The Producers," I was thrilled. I'd always liked him. And for a while that day, when I was young and inexperienced, I thought this was just his offbeat humor.

Then he yelled at a crew member and at Sam Falk, the *Times* photographer. Sidney Glazier, the producer, approached me. "Pray for me," he said.

Brooks went over to a cot and lay face down.

After I chatted with Zero Mostel and Gene Wilder, kind and funny men who cheered me up, I tried again with Mel Brooks. He still had no answers, just questions.

"What did you hope for when you came here? What did you want?"

I said I'd come with no preconceived notions.

"You must have had some idea. Or are you just a big blob of cotton...?"

As I headed for the door, he had one last question.

"Do you fool around?"

Back home, I wanted to cry, but wrote the piece instead. When it ran in *The Times* on Sunday, September 3, 1967, with a photo of Brooks yelling in mid-tirade, it got a lot of attention. Forty years later, when *Vanity Fair* mentioned it in their profile of Mel Brooks, I knew that my first freelance writing assignment was a lifetime lesson: writing well is our best revenge.

— *Joan Barthel*
   St.Louis, Missouri

I had been writing for years, as a newspaper reporter and freelancer, but I didn't really consider myself a capital-W "Writer" until my first book came out. Even then, it was tough to get past that question, "Oh, you're a *writer*. Well, how do you make a *living*?" But sweet vindication came my way about six months after *Haunted City*, a guide to New Orleans for Anne Rice fans, came out. I was back in the Crescent City researching a second edition. On the St. Charles Streetcar one afternoon, I saw a woman with her nose buried in . . . my book. I was stunned, too giddy to even whisper to her. I just drank in the euphoria of *seeing a stranger read my book*. Later that afternoon, I took an "Anne Rice" tour, which hadn't even existed when *Haunted City* first came out. The tour guide was snarky, trying to trip people up with really hard Anne Rice questions ... I knew the answers to all of them, of course, and couldn't help showing off a bit. One of the other tourists came up to me at some point and said, "Hey, you obviously love Anne Rice, you should read this book," and held up *Haunted City*. This time, I didn't choke: "I *wrote* that book," I replied, head held high. It was the best moment I've ever had as a writer, and that memory gets me writing when absolutely nothing else will work.

— *Joy Dickinson Tipping*
    Dallas, Texas

Take My Book—Please

I've spent 30 years as one-half of a happy couple with my honey, Peter. We've never married. With separate apartments, separate bedrooms, separate TV sets, and occasionally separate vacations, we've enjoyed the best of both worlds.

We've heard many times over the years that we're "unusual" and that we should "write a book!" Well, we have published articles about our relationship. We've talked about it on radio and TV. We started asking ourselves: Why are we putting ourselves out there without having something to sell? We were both published authors. We both had decent platforms—I was an editor at a national women's magazine, Peter worked at the biggest newspaper in New Jersey and appeared on TV weekly as a theater critic. Telling our story in book form seemed like the logical next step.

Except for one thing: No one wanted to publish it.

We wrote a great proposal. We got a good literary agent. We worked to build our platforms. But as we quickly learned, getting ourselves on TV or into the pages of a magazine was one thing; getting a book advance was another.

It's taken me the better part of two decades to absorb the harsh facts of book publishing, first as an author and now as an agent; namely, that book publishing follows—rather than sets—the trends. The book buyers who made He's Just Not That into You and Love Smart mega-sellers simply don't want to hear our message about love-without-marriage/love-with-independence. Fine. Go ahead, girls. Learn the hard way. There will be plenty of coping-with-divorce books out there when you're ready for them.

— *Linda Konner*
  New York, New York

Time Out(doors) With Tippi

"**W**alk faster, Shirley. That elephant is going to run over you."
My good friend and long-time photographer Ralph
Merlino's callus amusement annoyed me. It was easy for him to
talk. He was off to the side and of no special interest to the animal
in question.

Me? I was directly in front of the humongous creature. And, in
my hand, I carried the thing he most wanted in all the world at the
moment—a tiny box of Chiclets Chewing Gum.

We were on Actress Tippi Hedren's 180 acre Shambala Preserve,
home to some 70 lions, leopards, cougars and tigons (offspring of
unplanned tiger and lion matings) as well as two elephants and an
assortment of birds and waterfowl.

Earlier, I'd been jostled by an oversized tigress who was trying to
beat me through the gate of her own private yard, where Tippi had taken
me against my better judgment.

I was very glad when Tippi took the gum from me and tossed a
single tiny square into the cavernous mouth of her monstrous pet who
assumed an expression of utter bliss, proving a point Tippi was trying to
make.

This had been one of my scarier experiences of more than 150
celebrity interviews over some 20 years of at home with the stars stories.

— *Shirley Lee*
Chatsworth, California

Chapter 5
Seasoned Advice

On my first day as a newspaper reporter, an egregiously lazy copy editor unintentionally taught me the greatest lesson of my career.

My assignment involved an evening event at which a certain former governor of Texas was mentioned. We wrote for scanners in those days, using IBM typewriters and special magnetic ribbons. Correcting copy was a tedious and exacting process, involving a ruler and a magnetic-ink pen, no Whiteout allowed. I typed the story with no errors, or so I thought.

My two-take story appeared the next morning, under my byline, exactly as I'd written it—including my misspelling of John Connally's surname. I felt humiliated and pointed out my error to the copy editor. His reply, scatological expression omitted, was, "Your copy was so clean I just sent it through without reading it."

The lesson: Never submit anything to an editor that you wouldn't be proud to see under your byline. Assume every editor who handles your copy is as lazy as my first one.

I built a successful 30-year career on that premise. Repeat business is the secret of a freelancer's success. Others are more talented than I am, but no one is more of a perfectionist, and that learned trait has stood me in good stead. My reputation for submitting clean copy on time got around. As long as I worked as a journalist, my marketing consisted mostly of picking up the phone.

— *Miryam Ehrlich Williamson*
   Warwich, Massachusetts

Get Organized—and Boost Your Sales!

As a writer, I often feel like an air-traffic controller—sending a query to Editor A, a reprint to Editor B and a completed assignment to Editor C. The number of "planes in the air" would be difficult to juggle without my organizing secret: cheat sheets. They keep me sane. They might save your sanity, too. You'll need three types:

• Queries sent. Each query has its own spreadsheet, which notes how long a pitch has been with an editor, which editors have responded and when the idea is assigned.

• Article sales. Each article has its own sheet, which lists everywhere the article has sold. When a piece sells, I note which rights I've sold, and when I'll be able, per my contract, to resell it. When it's time to sell reprints, I track each sale and make sure I don't sell the piece to two competing publications.

• Annual income. This is my Grand Poobah of spreadsheets. But it's still simple. Every sale, from a $3,000 magazine assignment to a $50 reprint, goes here, categorized by publication. At year's end, this sheet goes to my accountant. It also helps me assess the health of my business over time.

It's a no-brainer: Setting up these simple spreadsheets will keep you organized, help you track your best income sources and article ideas and keep you from waking up at 2 a.m. wondering if you (oops!) accidentally sold the same reprint to *Augusta Family Magazine* and *Metro Augusta Parent*.

— *Kathy Sena*
   Manhattan Beach, California

"What Makes You Think You Can Write?"

Sound familiar? Sometimes the most defeating voices—those that stifle our creative juices—come from inside our own heads. Unfortunately these negative voices generally are as much a part of the creative process as the positive and productive voices are. You can't build a gorgeous building without uncovering some mud and dirt when you break ground, and you can't give birth to a gorgeous baby without intense labor pains. Likewise, you can't expect writing to be without its challenges.

Other times, the voices come from critics who question, among other things, your creativity. The truth is that desire and creativity generally come as a package deal. If you truly desire to write, then the creativity rests within you.

The real question is whether you are "brave" enough to be a writer. To be creative is to risk putting a part of yourself out there, for the world to see and criticize. It only follows that the protective part of you is going to go with it and keep saying, "Don't do it, don't do it."

I once read that God selected certain people to be writers, all the rest were left to play the role of critic. So let other people carry out their roles and you do yours, with the knowledge that the criticism and rejection will come. That means you've fulfilled your role.

— *Debra K. Traverso*
   Frederick, Maryland

I have struggled to discover my own creative voice since childhood, much to my mother's dismay as she washed my drawings and scribbles from numerous walls and laundered my finger painted party dresses.

As an adult I had to grow into my choices and make a living, which presented a fundamental artistic challenge. In my case this meant learning to conform to an academic style of writing that is apt to stifle creativity. Nonetheless, I developed a rather distinctive scholarly voice; but I gave up writing poetry and had little or no time for painting or drawing. This went on for many years. I even stopped writing fiction. It was as if my mind had been split in two and severed from my soul. Fortunately, writers and artists are born not made. Forms can be taught but formulas do not create art. Talent is innate and the real challenge is to discipline and train yourself so that you can access your imagination and express whatever is in you to say.

Walt Whitman, said, "stop this day and night with me and you shall possess the origin of all poems, You shall possess the good of the earth and sun. . . there are millions of suns left, you shall no longer take things at second or third hand." My wish for you is that you think for yourselves and make meaning out of your own true creativity.

— *Cassandra Langer*
  Jackson Heights, New York

Three Tips For Young Writers

I am one of those mythical beasts, a writer with a six-figure annual income. To what do I owe my success? From a journalistic career of 34 years (starting with a review of *Magnum Force* for my college newspaper), I offer these three tips:

Understand the supply chain. You are just one cog in a chain that creates a story, one that includes editors, copy editors, and designers. Remember those people when you submit your text. Include sources' contact information; provide fact-checking material, especially for obscure information; write leads that trigger graphic ideas. Don't be a prima donna if someone asks for the foregoing.

Maintain your network. In six years of freelancing full-time, I have gotten one assignment that wasn't a referral—and that was six years ago. If you're offered an assignment you can't handle, refer a colleague—they'll do the same for you. Even if you're fired, be professional—you will undoubtedly encounter your colleagues somewhere else, and they'll remember what you're like to work with.

Take assignments that stretch you. As the aphorism goes, do one thing each day that scares you. Whether it's tackling an article in a new industry or a new communication medium, such as Webcasting, you'll build up a broad repertoire. When someone asks if you have experience in a particular area, you can either say yes, or that you're willing to get it. After all, being a journalist means being able to cover new ideas first.

— *Howard Baldwin*
  Sunnyvale, California

Without realizing it, I learned the most important lesson of a writer's life—write what you know—when I was ten years old. My letter to the editor of *Western Horseman*, describing how it felt to ride a horse in the Arizona desert, was published. With my very first byline, a writer was hatched.

As a freelance writer for 28 years, this basic truth has stayed with me as I've reported from more than 120 countries (and counting). While I do plenty of profiles of others, and have had my share of "two experts and three anecdotes: it's a trend!" stories, it is the first-person piece I treasure most. At first, this felt selfish—who would want to read the details of my father's death, my allergy to Power Dressing in the 80s, the downside to dating younger men, the grief over the contents of a suitcase lost in 1990, the wisdom of my Aunt Mary's letters, why I care about high heels, or my post-traumatic stress battle after 9/11? But I was compelled to write about these things because they were what I knew, experiences and feelings that hit me where I lived. In the heart.

I know now this isn't selfish, know it by unexpected notes, e-mails, calls that tell me my words touch others. Surprise! We write what we know because somebody, somewhere is reading. By being true to our voices, we are connectors of the Human Experience. This is our gift to the world.

— *Mary Alice Kellogg*
  New York, New York

Taoist Gardening for Authors: A Guide to Surviving Difficult Editors

Recently, an editor behaved poorly to me. After pulling out handfuls of hair, I went out to garden. Working in the dirt calmed me; I got an "Aha!" Combine organic gardening with Taoism—the religion that practically invented "go with the flow"—and you've role models for remaining serene despite difficult editors!

Example: Taoists and natural gardeners employ minimal force. Bad editors are like garden pests: Using extreme measures to combat editorial destruction of your word-garden might also wipe out the good editors who keep your word-garden healthy.

When an editor called me at midnight, I risked editorial infestation not only of my manuscript, but of my life. While Mr. Caffeine left a message—he wanted to plant dull flowers in my word-garden, and weed out the best parts—I remembered Taoism's winning-by-laying-back. It was Mr. Caffeine's battle. I let him have it, all on his own, without any participation on my part: I didn't pick up the phone.

He tried to snare me with "Doing it your way will delay publication." That can strike terror in an author's heart. But gardeners plant lovely chives to ward off problematic bugs. Writers have their own wonderful "chives." Keep mental gardens worry-free! Do something so engaging that you can ignore publishing's inanities. Work on an additional book or plan a party.

Taoists and organic gardeners insist, "Sometimes, you *must* battle." And "Rally whatever forces needed." Stay calm, but know when it's time to phone your agent and announce, "We have a problem."

— *Francesca De Grandis*
Meadville, Pennsylvania

Once—very early in my career—I wrote a health article that appeared on the cover of a major national magazine. While in the production process, my editor asked me to inspect the galleys. I noticed that he had completely eliminated and re-written my lede (which I had worked hard on and thought was pretty awesome, by the way!). His "new, and improved version," in my opinion, was cliche and overdone. But my byline was on the article! I was so angry. Now, 20 years later, with 20/20 hindsight, I realize that was the beginning of my understanding of two things: 1) Never invest your ego in your writing and 2) Don't sweat the small stuff. Caveat emptor, new journalists!

— *Brianna Stevens, M.A.*
  Castro Valley, California

If you want to love writing, let your passion find you. I found my interest in writing early in my life and it took me into fascinating places. However, it wasn't until my passion found me that I really became immersed in my subjects; heathcare in general and women's health and menopause in particular. Back then, I was a hospital vice president for public affairs, writing and editing all the materials that were sent out of the institution. Then, at age fifty-one, I had a devastating menopause experience that my daughters still describe as the time "Mother went MIA—missing in action." Yes, I went to my physician who offered me valium instead of estrogen. That's when I got angry and realized that there was then a lack of understanding that fifteen percent of women have a terrible menopause experience, as did I, and that 70 percent of the others range between an easy time and a difficult one. I knew that when I felt better I would devote my writing life to making sure we women get good information and good healthcare. What followed was five books on the subject of women's midlife health, numerous articles and my ongoing column. To be thrilled as a writer, let your passion find you!

— *Ruth S. Jacobowitz*
  La Jolla, California

A Good Start

I studied journalism at the University of Illinois. In 1953 I took a magazine article writing course with Ted Peterson, an acerbic Kansan, tweed sport jacket, leather patches, the works, who later would write the definitive history of 20th Century American magazines. "Look at the person next to you," he said. "This semester one of you will sell an article." I turned to my neighbor and said, "He means you!" Ted's advice was succinct. "Study the magazine. Write a piece that looks, reads, and feels like what they publish." My first article was an interview with Soulima Stravinsky, a music faculty member, also Igor's son. I did a second on my pianist girlfriend improvising with dance students, then a third on a hot new technology, closed circuit television.

I sold Stravinsky to *The Etude* for $35 and the improvisers to *Music Journal* for $50. On a roll, I sent the TV piece to *Reader's Digest,* fantasizing $2,500 by return mail. (Yes, friends, relative rates were much higher then!) Instead, I got a personal rejection letter from Mary Steyn, the only editor whose name, thanks to a cosmic case of reverse senioritis, I recall five decades later. She wrote that the *Digest* had a similar piece on order. However, she liked my writing and wanted to encourage me. Shunted back to the minors, I sold the work to *Science Digest* for another $50. Some dozens of articles, three careers, and 10 books later, when young writers ask me how to publish, I channel the late Ted Peterson. "Study the magazine," I say. "I got that from the guy who studied all of them."

— *Marvin Weisbord*
  Wynnewood, Pennsylvania

After years of writing a successful television show and all that came with it—big buck salary, hobnobbing with celebrities, heavy-as-as brass knuckles Emmy, and a no-holds-barred expense account—I had the chutzpah to yearn for more. The desire driving me like a race car was the so-called real writer's life. I wanted to see my words in print, plus have time to shape my days. In a moment that flew on the gossamer wings of courage, I quit the cushy gig and bought an IBM selectric typewriter. Months went by while I sat at my desk in a cramped Greenwich Village apartment composing Susan Sontagesque essays nobody wanted. But one night, after a warm phone call from my long-distance lover, I let my mind drift to what was really going on in my life. Bad news: boyfriend far away. Good news: I didn't have to shave my legs. Off went the query to *Cosmopolitan Magazine*—and then forgotten. Two weeks later (those were the days editors answered queries promptly) my lover was in town and we were celebrating our good fortune when the phone rang. It was thin-as-a-stick of gum Helen herself on the line asking me to wade through Cosmo's book of leads. Dozens of assignments followed and from there I spring-boarded to plenty of other publications. Twenty years have passed, but I've never forgotten the lesson: to hear my true voice I have to listen to my heart.

    — *Robin Westen*
       Brooklyn, New York

So You Want to Be a Writer

I envy those who decided on a writerly career while still in school. For me, the first mammoth step came just before I turned 34. True, a desire to be a writer had niggled in the back of my mind for some years, but I'd never done anything about it.

To make ends meet, I sold ads by day and worked as a DJ at Radio KOHO by night. My wife waited tables part time to help. We were in a go nowhere situation. Somewhere, I got ahold of a *Writer's Digest* magazine, and an ad for a correspondence course that promised to teach me how to write articles and sell them caught my eye. I scraped the bottom of the budget barrel and came up with enough money to enroll.

One of the tips in the course was, watch the local newspaper for story ideas. And that's where my first article came from. I noticed an announcement that the director of the Honolulu Zoo had successfully bred back the Hawaiian Poi Dog. I sat right down at my portable Olympia and wrote a query letter to *Dog Fancy*. The magazine said okay. I interviewed the zoo director, took some photos, wrote up the article and sent it off.

A few weeks later, I got an acceptance. I'd learned how to turn news stories into magazine articles, a lesson that still serves me well today, hundreds of articles later.

— *Charles T. Whipple*
  Tokyo, Japan

Three Writing Secrets My Professors Never Taught Me (But Then, I Was A Math Major)

1. Rejection is fattening. Our first book, *Oh Lord, I Sound Just Like Mama* (with Esther Blumenfeld), took one year to write and, back when simultaneous submissions were unethical, four years to find a publisher. That first rejection letter read like a right jab to the stomach. I promptly ate three brownies. Jumbo brownies. If we had found a publisher that first month, I'd be a size 3. Or a 10.

2. Humor is a tough sell, even if you do everything right. We submitted the children's chapter to *Family Circle*, and it was rejected. However the editor-in-chief accidentally left her memos in our manuscript, and this is what we found: "Myrna: This is really funny, a great page for Mother's Day. Think we can get it for $500. Whattayathink??" And the response was, "Yes…but do we really need humor?"

3. Humor is funny…the funnier it is, the easier it looks. The work can't show, and we must be ruthless with our own creations. Here's the real reason God only wrote one bestseller: the editing process nearly killed His self-esteem. His first draft had 587 psalms, 79 commandments, and a Top 40 List of The Songs of Songs.

4. Just kidding. After studying calculus, differential equations and matrix algebra, I DID learn one thing from my math professor: Let the fame go and take the cash.

— *Lynne S. Alpern*
   Atlanta, Georgia

Musings on Downtimes

Enjoy your slow times; you'll miss them when you're busy. That's a truism of the freelance life, but it offered scant comfort during the perfect storm of 2001-2002. The economy started souring when the dot-com bubble burst. After 9/11, it flatlined. Health insurance premiums skyrocketed. Competition soared, too: suddenly every downsized editor was a writer.

A minority of freelancers, mainly medical writers, sailed serenely on. Others fell back on spousal safety nets. I had finished writing my second corporate history book, but when no new projects emerged I began working part-time as a paralegal for an elder-law firm. The work offered plenty of human interest. I kept my creativity alive through my "3Ps"—poetry, piano, and play-going.

Later I learned of ASJA colleagues who survived that dark time by substitute teaching, pet-sitting, or cashiering at Macy's or Trader Joe's. I wish more of us had admitted our situations publicly. I for one would have felt less alone. It was silly to take a global recession as a personal failure, but we did.

Writing business histories had taught me that smart companies treat crises as wake-up calls. The recession awakened me to the need to define my priorities, pursue them, and market more assertively. My Waterloo came when my lawyer bosses wanted to increase my hours to 19 per week (not 20, because then they'd have to provide benefits). Almost simultaneously, I landed a new history project. On the day I left the law firm I launched CorporateHistory.net, which has since produced several books.

I used to feel that if I wasn't writing, I wasn't working. In fact, we're business owners—and marketing is the real work at hand.

— *Marian Calabro*
   Hasbrouck Heights, New Jersey

Your 'Just Do It' Appointment

Researching markets, ugh.
    Checking statistics, ugh.
    Finding agents, ugh.
    Writing queries, ugh.
    Not selling, argh.

These are the steps so many writers hope to escape, skip over or avoid. But if you are dodging these tasks, then you're not selling. You may be bitching to anyone who will listen but you're not selling. "It's a bad market," you say.

Apathy reigns: I've been teaching e-courses online for a long time and there is one thing that writers fail at consistently—marketing. They'll spend years slogging through how-to books, taking great pains designing characters or nonfiction topics, attending conferences, but when it comes to selling, their brains stop.

They are often talented individuals who claim they love writing but they cannot wrap their mind around a market study or that they have to write to find their message.

The right words: People are getting published. The books on the market are not earthshaking, stunning or breathless prose. They're just stories, or how-tos, or semi-interesting topics. Until you start asking yourself: "What is the best approach? Is my audience definable and do I recognize their needs? Do I know who publishes my type of book? Am I understanding what this agent wants? Can I explain my book the way it needs to be told? Have I really analyzed the competition? Have I approached this as a business?

So you know what you must do, make an appointment to just do it.

— *Andrea Campbell*
  Hot Springs Village, Arizona

Writing from the Heart

I am a storyteller at heart and do best writing books. Respectable houses published ten of my books; the other two, *At The Mercy of Strangers: Growing Up on the Edge of the Holocaust* and *The Mothers' Group: Of Love, Loss and AIDS*, were self-published. It is these that I love best. It is some of their words that float into my consciousness when sleep eludes me, when I require comfort, when I need extra courage. Since these books deal with difficult periods of my life, people wonder whether their writing was painful.

It was not. While writing *Strangers* I was again the young girl dodging the Nazis during World War II. Today I smile at her innocence, am shocked at the risks I took, and am gladdened that she never, ever doubted that she would survive. Writing *The Mothers' Group* allowed me to spend time with my son. I vicariously cherished the times we spent together—on trips, at home, in restaurants and even in the hospital. I hated to let that book go to the printer; it was like losing David all over again.

It appears that for me good writing has to have a personal side, even if it is not always obvious. When writing about viruses, I was again the child suffering from endless middle ear infections. My pharmacist-father was watching, as I wrote the *Nurses Drug Handbook,* making sure that I explained everything properly; my Mom did the same for my book about *America's Art Museum.*

So, my advice to young writers is to write about subjects that have a personal relevance—even if it is far fetched.

— *Suzanne Loebl*
Mount Desert, Maine

The Stranger

I studied writing in college, and when a professor asked what type of career we planned I heard someone say, "published author." Yes, I thought, me too. But I never said it out loud. Instead I kept it to myself, and then after graduation proceeded to write advertising copy and to pen short stories never submitted. I eventually worked on other people's books, or sold them as a book-publishing employee for 10 years. My dream stayed secret.

Then I met an old man at the Los Angeles convention center. It was a random encounter (or so I thought). This old guy must have been in his 80s. He was stretching his legs, taking a break from a U.S. citizen ceremony he was attending for a relative. I was there working a photo concession—yet another non-writing diversion. The elderly man was quite friendly, but suddenly grew serious. For some reason he confessed to me his biggest regret in life. He told me he always planned on writing books, but somehow he was always too busy, and never found the time to start. After all, he'd had a family to support. His eyes looked down sadly.

Of course I never forgot this man.

Soon I attended an ASJA conference (my people!) and learned how to become a member. Today I await publication of "Plantations and Historic Homes of New Orleans," my fourth book. The lesson? Begin what you long to do NOW, and persevere.

— *Jan Arrigo*
  Slidell, Louisiana

Chapter 6
Why ASJA Matters

For 25 years working as a freelance writer, I never considered joining a writers' association. In fact I wasn't aware that writers, as a group, associated. Or maybe I didn't need to know, since I had Linda, the perfect writing partner, to whom I turned whenever I needed help with excess work, marketing leads, editing, or motivation.

Four years ago, when Linda was diagnosed with ALS (Lou Gehrig's Disease), I promised to visit her every Thursday evening until the end. As always, she was inspirational, not only facing her illness with courage and curiosity, but also challenging me to learn from it and grow as both a person and a writer. Throughout my career, she was my greatest supporter and pushed me to take risks I might never have taken on my own. When she died last summer, I found myself considering a change of careers. I was too aware of the void.

But not writing wasn't an option, as Linda understood. While she was still able to communicate, she emailed me a link to asja.org and encouraged me to attend the next meeting. I did and over the next year went to several more. Last year I joined the association and have realized that, as with friendship, the more you put into it, the more you get out. We've all taken different paths to arrive at the point where we find partnership amongst other writers. I'm so grateful that my friend pointed me in this direction.

— *Lisa Stockwell*
  Sebastopol, California

Truth wins, so never quit

All professional writers experience disappointment, rejection, setbacks, criticism, and losses. They are as much a part of our careers as are successes and awards, even the unexpected collateral rewards of helping make the world a better place.

Sometimes, however, the losses appear so great they are seemingly irrecoverable: Seemingly is the optimum word here, because all things are recoverable. All setbacks and disappointments may be turned to victory if only we view unfortunate circumstances, not as problems, but as challenges and opportunities.

In my career I've experienced all of the above, including one—a series of propagandized attacks against my work and credibility widely spread throughout the mainstream media (and since proven to be engineered by a foreign terrorist organization)—that seemed irrecoverable.

There is no way I can detail what happened in the short space I have here. So let me instead leave you all—especially the up-and-coming writers—with a few snippets of what I learned from my great "challenge" that will always serve you well no matter what you encounter in this very tough business.

First, many writers have enemies at some level—either professional or political (and, as in my case, real wartime bad guys). Second, truth is light; and enemies will often go to great lengths to extinguish that light. Third, there is nothing in this business or this world that can ever defeat you if you always hold on to the truth as you would a small child in a hailstorm. Fourth, don't despair because truth ultimately surfaces. And lastly, as Churchill purportedly said, "Never, never, never quit."

— *W. Thomas Smith Jr.*
Columbia, South Carolina

My ASJA Memory

While an assistant editor for *The Kiwanis Magazine*, I became aware of the Society of Magazine Writers through freelance writers selling to that publication, including Joseph Bell, Dick Dunlop and Al Balk.

Lowly positioned, I observed my boss escort these privileged persons past my desk into an inner sanctum, later to emerge with writing assignments. They also were taken to lunch. Nobody ever took me to lunch.

It occurred to me that if I wanted to get rich and eat free lunches, I needed to quit my job and become a freelance magazine writer. I eventually tendered my resignation, but before departing secured an invitation to the Chicago SMW branch's monthly meeting at Riccardo's Restaurant. However, I had not sold anything yet! No credits. No reason why any editor might offer an assignment, except on speculation, which we all know is the road to perdition.

Then, the afternoon I was due to attend my first SMW meeting, I received a call from my wife. *Parent's Magazine* had just accepted my essay, "We Had Our Baby—Naturally." They paid $250, more money then than it is now.

This allowed me to walk into my meeting with Joe and Dick and Al and other SMW members proudly, with a proper response if anyone asked, "What have you sold recently?" Nobody asked, but I am sure I mentioned that fact at some point during dinner.

That was 1959, and I continue to be a proud member of the SMW, now ASJA.

— *Hal Higdon*
  Long Beach, Indiana

There's plenty of angst, shtick, rage, stealing, terror, worry and waiting in the writing game, but very little of that comes from other writers. I've never seen an occupation where colleagues are so generous and encouraging. Nineteen books ago, I was working on my second book, which happened to be about diabetes: it was before Google—who knew anything about diabetes? I never had it nor knew anyone who did. I was so young I hardly knew anyone who ever had a migraine. One morning, the doorbell rang and there was ASJA member Joan Heilman with an armful of books, papers and good interview names on, what else, diabetes: she'd just finished her own book on the subject and was offering me every bit of her research. I hardly knew her.

I thought I'd never forget that kindness. I never did.

Try saying that for any other field.

— *Sherry Suib Cohen*
   New York, New York

ASJA has 60 years worth of stories, but I've only been a member for a mere two years. I became a member just before two conferences ago, and at the time I joined, I was more journalist than author, but I yearned to be the latter. The first conference was a doozy—but in the best sense: I received not one, but two book contracts, as well as two contacts that led to two stories. Last year's conference was also profitable: it led to my third and fourth book contracts. I've only been freelancing for five years, and ASJA is one of the big things that has led from being a just making it freelance writer and wannabe author to an actual author and a freelancer who just turned down three assignments. No doubt, ASJA is one of the best things I've ever done for my career.

— *Jeanette Hurt*
   Milwaukee, Wisconsin

Transforming ASJA into a National Organization

Freelance writing is not for the faint of heart. It is only for those who prefer autonomy to safety, self-motivation to the dictates of others. It is also for those with a capacity for solitude but who have the wisdom to join hands with other like-minded souls, drawing strength and knowledge from their insights and experience.

When I left my full-time job to freelance I was already a member of ASJA. I gained so much from the organization (writing assignments through Dial-A-Writer, knowledge about markets and contracts, new friends and colleagues) that, eventually, I felt the desire to "give back." I became president of ASJA during a period of tremendous technological change. The arrival of email communication helped transform what was once a New York-centric organization into a national one.

I am proud to say that I supported bringing in non-East Coast board members and nominated the first West Coast Vice President who, when I stepped down, became ASJA's first non-New York President. I also encouraged many technological changes to our newsletter which allowed it to be written and edited from anywhere in the U.S. For ASJA, these were revolutionary steps. It was, at times, a bumpy transition but, in retrospect, it enabled ASJA to grow, thrive, and draw on the amazing talents of its members, regardless of where they reside. I am tremendously proud of my role in that transition which, difficult though it was, set the stage for the vitality of ASJA today and tomorrow.

— *Eleanor Foa Dienstag*
New York, New York

Every Thursday for twelve years, ASJA members Barbara Bartocci, Deborah Shouse, and I have met at 7 a.m. at Homer's Coffee Shop in Overland Park, Kansas. Whatever the weather, we're there for two hours for what we simply call "Writers," as in, "See you at Writers."

We've settled on Homer's because it's friendly and quiet and serves wonderful pots of steeped tea. We've settled on each other because all three of us make our livings writing nonfiction, and because we have found in each other simpatico writing partners. We edit each other's work, help each other stay on deadline, moan about and praise our editors, think up titles, brainstorm future projects, give pep talks, and pat each other on the back. We have also assisted each other in the transition from magazine to book work.

Other writers have asked to join us. It's hard to say no, but we have learned that three is a perfect size, given the intensity of our work. If anything, we could lengthen our meeting time. Indeed, sometimes we request editing help between sessions.

I think the secret to our longevity is that with time we have become sensitive editors of each other's distinctive styles and message. Because of each other, we are better, and more successful, writers. And we take time each week to share our personal lives, offering each other the same support we do with our writing. Our friendship is deep and precious.

This Thursday at 7, you'll know where to find us.

— *Andrea Warren*
   Prairie Village, Kansas

Not So Funny Tidings

Humor, especially satire isn't easy to sell. Nonetheless, after selling two satirical pieces to *Esquire* early in my career I thought that maybe I had found a niche. I was wrong.

Some time later, after selling several non-humor pieces to the SAS Magazine, *Scanorama,* I pitched my editor on a satirical piece about gloom merchants, people who sold kitchy merchandise commemorating dead heroes. Told to go ahead, I wrote the piece and sent it off immediately. The response—by airmail in pre-email days—accompanied by a check was more than I could have anticipated. They loved the piece and, as the letter said, it marked the first time that three editors laughed aloud at the same meeting.

Months went by, and I was still waiting for the article to appear. Then, at last, a letter arrived from the magazine with a new editor's signature. Well, after I had received payment and deposited the check in my bank, I was told that my submission wasn't suitable for the magazine. What, I wondered, happened to the laughing editors?

Thanks to ASJA, however, my faith in humor writing returned. At a monthly dinner meeting, I casually asked an editor from *Family Health* if she might be interested in a satire on the then-prevalent water shortage, which had been jingling around in my mind for some time. Without a definite commitment, I wrote the article the next day and sent it in. Within days a check arrived and, more importantly, I never received a letter telling me my piece wasn't suitable. The article was published several months later. No wonder I enjoyed going to AJSA meetings.

— *Alvin H. "Skip" Reiss*
  New York, New York

I got my first rejection letter when I was 15 from Harvey Kurtzman, the founder of *Mad Magazine*, and my second, a year or so later, from *The Village Voice*. Undaunted, I plunged into journalism, working for three newspapers, the *New York Herald Tribune*, the *Philadelphia Bulletin*, and the *Washington Post*. It's worth noting, I suppose, that two of those three papers no longer exist and the third, where I spent 34 years as a reporter and editor, is struggling to survive in the Internet age. For aging inked stain wretches like me, it seems like a good time to be on the outside looking in. The bittersweet corollary of newspaper decline is the rise of freelancing. In January 2004, I joined the ranks and soon also joined ASJA. I'd always done some freelancing "on the outside," in what I referred to as "my copious spare time." My freelancing usually came during periods of heightened frustration with my employer. But I always wanted to do more and so welcomed the opportunity, when it came, to do so. So far, it's been more than so good. I've built up a substantial freelance business, have picked up a couple of awards along the way, and through ASJA have made new friends and colleagues who, in ASJA forums and conferences, have been kind and generous in sharing information and contacts. If as Stephen King has written, "The so-called 'writing life' is basically sitting on your ass," ASJA is a nice cushion.

— *Gene Meyer*
   Silver Spring, Maryland

On a research trip to Los Angeles in 1989, I looked up Isobel Silden in the ASJA directory. She immediately invited me to lunch and asked how she could help me. My first book, *Sixth Sense*, was coming out in 6 months. Isobel couldn't wait for us to finish eating lunch. She jumped up and began working the phones to line up interested reporters, editors, and talk show hosts. "Your book will be a huge hit in this town," she said, adding that intuition was one of her favorite topics.

One of her phone calls that day was to Kathleen Doheny, a reporter for the *Los Angeles Times*. Not only did she write a front-page article for the "View" section about my book, Kathy and I became lifelong friends.

Isobel was diagnosed with lung cancer in 1990. Although I don't remember when she died, it seems less important to me than remembering her as my mentor/guardian angel. Isobel's professional caring and genrosity exemplifies the best that ASJA has to offer.

— *Laurie Nadel*
New York, New York

There is no organization like ASJA. It is the gold standard for writers, and very useful to all of us.

— *Joanne Prim Shade*
Chicago, Illinois

I first heard about the Society of Magazine Writers (now ASJA) in 1967 from Richard Dunlop, a member whose article-writing workshop I attended in Winnetka, Illinois. Dick encouraged me to submit a story to *McCall's*, which it bought for its regional section; then I sold front-of-the-book pieces to *Redbook* and *Good Housekeeping*. By the following year I had accumulated enough credits to join the Society, and in 1969 when I went to my first dinner meeting, I happened to sit next to Mort Weisinger, best known as the editor of *Superman* but also a prolific and successful freelancer.

Mort drove me home (we were both living on Long Island), then took me under his cape and became my mentor and friend. When I had questions about this crazy business I called him, when I had successes I called him, when I wrote queries for magazine pieces I ran them past him. One day I was in the dumps after I had received go-aheads on two queries to two major women's magazines—and then got rejections and kill fees for both articles. After I moaned and threatened to go back to working at a *real* job, Mort made me laugh with this: "You know how the Directory lists specialties for all the members—you can list your specialty as query letters!"

Then when I had cover-line articles for six months in a row in *Redbook, Reader's Digest, Seventeen*, and *Ladies' Home Journal*, Mort kvelled over me as if he had been my mother. He was my first good friend in ASJA—but not my last.

— *Sally Wendkos Olds*
  Port Washington, New York

Sometime in the early 1980s, when I had been in ASJA for just a few years, I accepted the invitation to join D.C. ASJA members on a special tour of NPR studios. I drove into Washington and parked close by. I remember talking with fellow member Lynne Lamberg and watching Corey Flintoff cue in the music after the news.

A few of us decided to go out afterwards for an early dinner in nearby Chinatown. We sat at a big round table, laughing and eating. I was young, barely published, and I loved the feeling of almost belonging to this group of smart people who made their living by the word.

We walked out together, thank goodness, because when I got to my parking place, the curb was bare. Now I noticed that faded street sign: "No Parking After 5 p.m." It was five to seven. I fumbled around at a pay phone but a recording on the 800 number said the office closed at seven.

And here's the point of this story. Pat McNees, whom I had never met before, invited me to stay overnight in her apartment. She gave me the sofa and I got a few hours' rest, then tiptoed out early to get a cab to the impoundment lot, where I liberated my car. Luckily, I hadn't quite maxed out my Visa. But I'll bet if I had really needed it, Pat would have loaned me the $75, too. That's just how ASJA members are.

— *Susan Tyler Hitchcock*
Covesville, Virginia

ASJA has been a very important part of my personal and professional life since I joined in my early twenties. On a personal level, especially during my single years (till 36), ASJA was very much of an extended family to me. I met one of my dear friends at an ASJA conference during those early years; our friendship has endured over the decades. I more recently reconnected with my college roommate and old friend after decades when we recognized each other at the registration desk for the All Member's Day in 2007.

Being a member of ASJA has also had numerous professional benefits. I will only cite a few outstanding examples; I heard about, competed for, and landed a visiting professorship in nonfiction writing at Penn State University through what used to be called Dial-a-Writer. More recently, an ASJA member shared through the ASJA Freelance Writers Search that his agent was looking for a time management expert to a new book. I applied, the agent and publisher chose me to write the book, and that book, my third on the topic, entitled *Work Less, Do More*, will be published by Sterling Publishing Company on September 2, 2008.

Throughout my freelance magazine, book, and online writing career, covering topics including friendship, getting help, and crime victims, being a member of ASJA has been a positive constant.

— *Jan Yager, Ph.D. (the former J.L./Janet/ Barkas)*
Stamford, Connecticut

Congratulations, ASJA, on your sixtieth anniversary!

For six decades you have served as parent, teacher and cheerleader for those of us called to the writing life, that irrepressible drive to preserve human behavior on the page and now on the screen. Today, while you, ASJA, are approaching senior citizen status, you are as nimble and savvy as when you were first born—perhaps even more so, as you matured into America's premier nonfiction writers' organization.

In spite of your sixty years, you will never grow old, for your spirit remains perpetually young.

It is to you, ASJA, that I have always turned in moments of self-doubt and uncertainty—between books, while searching for new journalist markets, and as a guide to the latest publishing trends.

Like a trusted friend, you have also been there in moments of triumph. When I have published articles and books and won awards, you and your membership have celebrated with me. Indeed, several of those awards even emanated from you. For me, as for hundreds of other ASJA writers who have evolved from fledgling writers to seasoned authors and journalists, you remain a beloved parent—reliable, nurturing, wise.

In today's rapidly evolving media marketplace, what more could a writer want?

ASJA, I wish you long life and pride, for you have made this world a better place for me, for countless other writers and for that literary muse who perpetually hovers over us, insisting that we preserve human experience through the power of words.

— *Nancy Rubin Stuart*
New York, New York

About ASJA

Founded in 1948, the American Society of Journalists and Authors is the nation's leading organization of independent nonfiction writers. Our membership consists of more than 1,100 outstanding freelance writers of magazine articles, trade books, and many other forms of nonfiction writing, each of whom has met ASJA's exacting standards of professional achievement.

ASJA brings leadership in establishing professional and ethical standards, and in recognizing and encouraging the pursuit of excellence in nonfiction writing. The Association is a primary voice in representing freelancers' interests, serving as spokesman for their right to control and profit from uses of their work in the new media and otherwise.

ASJA headquarters are in New York City. The Society has active regional chapters in Northern and Southern California, the Rocky Mountain area, and Washington, DC.

Writers Emergency Assistance Fund

The Writers Emergency Assistance Fund (formerly the Llewellyn Miller Fund) is administered through the ASJA Charitable Trust, which has 501(c)(3) tax-exempt status. Its mission is to help established freelance writers across the country who, because of advanced age, illness, disability, a natural disaster, or an extraordinary professional crisis are unable to work. A writer need not be a member of ASJA to qualify for a grant.

Since 1982, the Fund has issued more than 150 grants. Among the recipients have been writers representing diverse backgrounds and interests, with an impressive list of honors and credentials among them. Each year numbers of such talented and deserving people appeal to the Writers Emergency Assistance Fund. For many, the Fund represents their last hope for help. Contributions are fully tax-deductible, and can be made online or by check.

Freelance Writer Search

The Freelance Writer Search is a service of the American Society of Journalists and Authors that helps publishers, agents, media, and corporations reach the best freelance writers, editors and editorial project managers in America who are capable of handling any assignment on time and within budget. Not only a great resource for those looking for talent, it has enabled many ASJA members to connect with new markets for their writing. Accessible online at http://www.freelancewritersearch.com/

🕯 🕯 🕯

Past Presidents of ASJA

Maurice Zolotow
Temple Fielding
Donald Robinson
Morton Sontheimer
James Poling
Robert L. Heilbroner
Morton Hunt
Jack Harrison Pollack
Lawrence Lader
Murray Teigh Bloom
Vance Packard
Gerald Walker
Bernard Asbell
Robert Bendiner
Norman M. Lobsenz
Jean Libman Block
Thomas J. Fleming
William Surface
Alfred Balk
Theodore Irwin
Jhan Robbins
Lin Root
David R. Zimmerman
Terry Morris

Patrick M. McGrady, Jr.
Mort Weisinger
Ruth Winter
Dian Dincin Buchman
Grace W. Weinstein
Sally Wendkos Olds
June Roth
John H. Ingersoll
Evelyn Kaye
Dodi Schultz
Glen Evans
David W. Kennedy
Thomas Bedell
Katharine Davis Fishman
Florence Isaacs
Mark L. Fuerst
Janice Hopkins Tanne
Claire Safran
Eleanor Foa Dienstag
Samuel Greengard
Jim Morrison
Lisa Collier Cool
Jack El-Hai
Robert Bittner

Barnes & Noble
proudly salutes the

AMERICAN
SOCIETY OF
JOURNALISTS
AND AUTHORS

on its
60th Anniversary